INTRODUCING
ISSUES
OPPOSING
VIEWPOINTS

D0861123

Legalization of Marijuana

M. M. Eboch, Book Editor

GREENHAVEN
PUBLISHING

Published in 2020 by Greenhaven Publishing, LLC
353 3rd Avenue, Suite 255, New York, NY 10010

Articles in Greenhaven Publishing anthologies are often edited for length to meet page requirements. In addition, original titles of these works are changed to clearly present the main thesis and to explicitly indicate the author's opinion. Every effort is made to ensure that Greenhaven Publishing accurately reflects the original intent of the authors. Every effort has been made to trace the owners of the copyrighted material.

Library of Congress Cataloging-in-Publication Data

Names: Eboch, M. M., editor.
Title: Legalization of marijuana / M. M. Eboch, book editor
Description: New York : Greenhaven Publishing, 2020. | Series: Introducing issues with opposing viewpoints | Includes bibliographical references and index. | Audience: Grades 7-12.
Identifiers: LCCN 2019023832 | ISBN 9781534506695 (library binding) | ISBN 9781534506688 (paperback)
Subjects: LCSH: Marijuana—Law and legislation—United States—Juvenile literature.
Classification: LCC KF3891.M2 .L44 2020 | DDC 344.7304/233—dc23
LC record available at https://lccn.loc.gov/2019023832

Manufactured in the United States of America

Website: http://greenhavenpublishing.com

Contents

Foreword

I ndulging in a wide spectrum of ideas, beliefs, and perspectives is a critical cornerstone of democracy. After all, it is often debates over differences of opinion, such as whether to legalize abortion, how to treat prisoners, or when to enact the death penalty, that shape our society and drive it forward. Such diversity of thought is frequently regarded as the hallmark of a healthy and civilized culture. As the Reverend Clifford Schutjer of the First Congregational Church in Mansfield, Ohio, declared in a 2001 sermon, "Surrounding oneself with only like-minded people, restricting what we listen to or read only to what we find agreeable is irresponsible. Refusing to entertain doubts once we make up our minds is a subtle but deadly form of arrogance." With this advice in mind, Introducing Issues with Opposing Viewpoints books aim to open readers' minds to the critically divergent views that comprise our world's most important debates.

Introducing Issues with Opposing Viewpoints simplifies for students the enormous and often overwhelming mass of material now available via print and electronic media. Collected in every volume is an array of opinions that captures the essence of a particular controversy or topic. Introducing Issues with Opposing Viewpoints books embody the spirit of nineteenth-century journalist Charles A. Dana's axiom: "Fight for your opinions, but do not believe that they contain the whole truth, or the only truth." Absorbing such contrasting opinions teaches students to analyze the strength of an argument and compare it to its opposition. From this process readers can inform and strengthen their own opinions, or be exposed to new information that will change their minds. Introducing Issues with Opposing Viewpoints is a mosaic of different voices. The authors are statesmen, pundits, academics, journalists, corporations, and ordinary people who have felt compelled to share their experiences and ideas in a public forum. Their words have been collected from newspapers, journals, books, speeches, interviews, and the Internet, the fastest growing body of opinionated material in the world.

Introducing Issues with Opposing Viewpoints shares many of the well-known features of its critically acclaimed parent series, Opposing

Viewpoints. The articles allow readers to absorb and compare divergent perspectives. Active reading questions preface each viewpoint, requiring the student to approach the material thoughtfully and carefully. Photographs, charts, and graphs supplement each article. A thorough introduction provides readers with crucial background on an issue. An annotated bibliography points the reader toward articles, books, and websites that contain additional information on the topic. An appendix of organizations to contact contains a wide variety of charities, nonprofit organizations, political groups, and private enterprises that each hold a position on the issue at hand. Finally, a comprehensive index allows readers to locate content quickly and efficiently.

Introducing Issues with Opposing Viewpoints is also significantly different from Opposing Viewpoints. As the series title implies, its presentation will help introduce students to the concept of opposing viewpoints and learn to use this material to aid in critical writing and debate. The series' four-color, accessible format makes the books attractive and inviting to readers of all levels. In addition, each viewpoint has been carefully edited to maximize a reader's understanding of the content. Short but thorough viewpoints capture the essence of an argument. A substantial, thought-provoking essay question placed at the end of each viewpoint asks the student to further investigate the issues raised in the viewpoint, compare and contrast two authors' arguments, or consider how one might go about forming an opinion on the topic at hand. Each viewpoint contains sidebars that include at-a-glance information and handy statistics. A Facts About section located in the back of the book further supplies students with relevant facts and figures.

Following in the tradition of the Opposing Viewpoints series, Greenhaven Publishing continues to provide readers with invaluable exposure to the controversial issues that shape our world. As John Stuart Mill once wrote: "The only way in which a human being can make some approach to knowing the whole of a subject is by hearing what can be said about it by persons of every variety of opinion and studying all modes in which it can be looked at by every character of mind. No wise man ever acquired his wisdom in any mode but this." It is to this principle that Introducing Issues with Opposing Viewpoints books are dedicated.

Introduction

"Supporters of legalization mention its perceived health benefits, or see it as no more dangerous than other drugs. To opponents, it is a dangerous drug, one that inflicts damage on people and society more generally."
—*Pew Research Center, April 14, 2015*

Marijuana is the most commonly used illegal drug in the United States. That may not be true for long, as more states vote to legalize marijuana. Voters are demonstrating that the majority of them—at least in some regions—see marijuana as fairly harmless or even beneficial. Yet the federal government still classifies marijuana as a Schedule I drug, as dangerous as heroin, LSD, or meth. According to the DEA, marijuana has "no currently accepted medical use and a high potential for abuse."

Marijuana, also called cannabis, pot, and many other names, has a long history of use. Ancient cultures may have used the plant in religious ceremonies for it psychoactive properties, also known as its high. However, this early cannabis had low levels of THC, which is the chemical that creates mind-altering effects. The plant was popular for other reasons: it was easy to grow, grew quickly, and had many uses. Hemp fiber from the plant was used to make clothing, sails, rope, and paper. Hemp seeds are highly nutritious and do not contain THC. Early colonists in America often grew hemp for its many practical uses.

Marijuana has also been praised for its medicinal qualities for millennia. In Asia, it was used as an herbal medicine by around 500 BCE. In the 1830s, an Irish doctor studying in India discovered that cannabis extracts could lessen stomach pain and vomiting. By the late 1800s, pharmacies and doctors' offices throughout Europe and the US offered cannabis extracts.

So why did attitudes change?

In the early 1900s, Mexican immigrants introduced the idea of smoking marijuana for enjoyment. During the Great Depression, widespread unemployment led to a backlash against immigrants. At the same time, the prohibition movement viewed all mind-altering substances as dangerous. By 1931, twenty-nine states had outlawed cannabis.

In the 1960s, many young people experimented with mind-altering substances. Drugs became a symbol of rebellion and political dissent. This led to the government's "war on drugs." In 1970, the Controlled Substances Act made marijuana completely illegal nationwide.

Today, many people feel that marijuana is no worse than alcohol or cigarettes. Therefore, they argue, it should have the same restrictions, but no more. Some argue that the war on drugs has failed. It has overwhelmed the court systems, it costs taxpayers billions of dollars, and it has filled our prisons with people arrested for the possession of small amounts of marijuana. With a felony drug conviction, these people may struggle to ever get decent jobs. Additionally, many argue that the war on drugs is also racist. African Americans and white Americans use marijuana at about the same rates, yet African Americans are almost four times more likely than whites to be arrested for marijuana-related offenses. Moreover, the war on drugs has failed to reduce marijuana use and availability. If the war on drugs has failed, some see legalization as a better option.

Interest in medical marijuana has also grown. It is often used to treat anxiety and to reduce nausea from cancer treatments. Many other claims have been made about marijuana. It can allegedly prevent Alzheimer's, stop cancer cells from spreading, relieve arthritis, protect the brain, and even improve lung health. But are these claims actually true?

As a Schedule I drug, little research has been permitted on marijuana. Many of the medical claims are unproven. Even if marijuana has medical uses, some argue that drugs should be made in a lab. Smoking pot or eating marijuana edibles is not a reliable way to get an accurate dose. The government does not regulate marijuana, so its quality and consistency are not controlled. It may contain other harmful substances.

As for recreational use, marijuana may be no more harmful than alcohol. But alcohol leads to thousands of deaths every year, many through drunk driving or other accidents. Should we allow another mind-altering substance that is also associated with a higher risk of accidents?

In any case, not everyone agrees that marijuana is harmless. The amount of THC in marijuana has increased dramatically as growers cultivate more potent strains. That means the effects can be more dramatic. Some of those effects are pleasurable, but high doses can cause hallucinations, delusions, and psychosis. Even moderate doses may interfere with thinking, problem solving, and memory. In the long term, marijuana use can affect brain development. It can interfere with learning, thinking, and memory, even cause a long-term lowering of one's IQ. Teenagers and young adults, whose brains have not fully developed, are especially at risk. They may never recover the lost brain function.

In recent years, many states have changed their laws about marijuana. Some allow only medicinal cannabis, while others allow adults to use marijuana for recreational purposes. Overall, the trend seems to be toward loosening restrictions on marijuana at the state level. Yet the federal government still considers cannabis illegal, and people may be arrested for its possession or use, even when it is legal in their state.

For all the claims about marijuana, there's a lot we don't know. Should the drug be reclassified to allow for more research? Should it be legalized nationwide? If so, how can we reduce the risks? Or do the dangers outweigh the potential benefits, meaning marijuana should remain illegal?

Exploring the issues through research, philosophical discussions, and personal experience can help individuals determine their answer. The current debates are explored in *Introducing Issues with Opposing Viewpoints: Legalization of Marijuana*, shedding light on this contemporary issue.

Chapter 1

Are There Benefits to Legalizing Marijuana?

The cannabis plant is the source of the drug marijuana.

Marijuana May Be Safer Than Alcohol

"The overall take-home message may be if you are about to drive a car, if you are an adolescent, or you are pregnant you probably should not use either one."

Lauren Villa

In the following viewpoint, the author compares marijuana to alcohol. Experts and the public debate about which is the more dangerous substance. In several of the aspects considered here, alcohol is more dangerous than marijuana. However, both have the potential to cause harm. Additionally, teenagers and pregnant women may be more at risk. The author argues that no one should drive while under the influence of either substance. Overall, this viewpoint says marijuana is not more harmful than alcohol, despite the fact that marijuana is illegal and alcohol is not. Lauren Villa has a Master's in Public Health from the University of California, Berkeley.

AS YOU READ, CONSIDER THE FOLLOWING QUESTIONS:

1. Is alcohol or marijuana more likely to lead directly to death, according to this viewpoint?
2. What are the risks of driving under the influence of alcohol or marijuana?
3. How do alcohol and marijuana affect memory?

"The Great Debate: Alcohol vs Marijuana," by Lauren Villa, DrugAbuse.com. Reprinted by permission.

You may have had the debate yourself—what's worse? Alcohol or marijuana? With new studies coming out, more laws legalizing the recreational, and medicinal use of marijuana, the conversation seems to come up again and again.

Even though we may all have different opinions, marijuana remains a Schedule I drug, while alcohol is legal to consume for people who are 21 years of age or older.

In a now famous *New Yorker* interview, President Obama said, "I don't think it [marijuana] is more dangerous than alcohol."

So, is alcohol or marijuana more dangerous? Here we present both sides of the debate so you can decide for yourself.

Overdose

In most cases, drinking alcohol is not life-threatening. However, when people consume too much alcohol, it can be fatal. The CDC reports that nearly 88,000 alcohol-related deaths occur each year. And binge drinking accounted for about half of these deaths.

In comparison, the number of deaths caused by marijuana is almost zero. A study found that a fatal dose of TCH, the potent chemical in marijuana, would be between 15 and 70 grams. To give you an idea of how much marijuana that is, consider that a typical joint contains about half a gram of marijuana. That means that you would have to smoke between 238 and 1,113 joints in a day to overdose on marijuana. That's a lot of joints.

Crime Rates

When it comes to what substance will put someone at risk for getting hurt or hurting others, alcohol is considered to cause the most harm.

A study on marijuana use and intimate partner violence found that couples who used marijuana had lower rates of intimate partner violence in the first 9 years of marriage. In fact, men who used marijuana were the least likely to commit an act of intimate partner violence against a spouse.

Though alcohol is legal, there are some restrictions on its consumption, prohibiting minors from drinking and driving while intoxicated.

Driving

Driving stoned is considerably safer than driving drunk, but it is still dangerous.

Besides alcohol, marijuana is the most commonly detected drug in drivers involved in car accidents. One study found that marijuana increased the odds of being in [a] car accident by 83%.

You may think that 83% is high, but when alcohol was involved, the odds of being in a car accident increased more than 2,200%!

When *both* alcohol and drugs were in the system, the risk of having a fatal car accident is especially high.

What's the takeaway here? It's never a good idea to drive under the influence of drugs *or* alcohol, but especially both.

Learning and Memory

After a long night of heavy drinking, you may not remember what happened the night before. This is often referred to as a "blackout."

When you drink heavily it can impair your ability to create new memories. Over 50% of frequent binge drinkers reported at least one time in the past year when they blacked out and forgot where they were or what they did when they were drinking.

In an email survey, college students reported that after a blackout they did things that they could not remember, like driving drunk, having unprotected sex, or engaged in risky behavior.

Along the lines of memory, recent studies have shown that adolescents who smoke marijuana may be at greater risk for problems with memory and learning later in life. The studies remain inconclusive about how much marijuana use causes impairments of learning and memory. But studies have demonstrated that these types of changes in the brain may increase the risk of psychological difficulties later in life.

Controversy remains over what percentage of psychosis risk can be linked to marijuana use and how much depends on a person's genetics.

Pregnancy

Using alcohol even during the first few weeks of pregnancy can cause long-lasting effects on a child. According to the CDC, 3.3 million women are at risk of exposing their baby to alcohol.

If you drink during pregnancy, you are at risk for having a child born with physical, behavioral, and intellectual disabilities—these are called fetal alcohol spectrum disorders (FASDs). According to the CDC there is no known amount of alcohol that is safe to consume during pregnancy.

But marijuana may not be safe either. Studies show there may be a link between marijuana use during pregnancy and low birth weight. Despite marijuana being the most commonly used illegal drug during pregnancy, it's hard to tell what the effect of marijuana use is, since there are not many studies out there.

So you're probably wondering, with all of this information the question remains, alcohol or marijuana? What side are you on? Perhaps we can shift our thinking and instead of taking sides, we can all agree that both alcohol and marijuana have their risks. The overall take-home message may be if you are about to drive a car, if you are an adolescent, or you are pregnant you probably should not use either one.

EVALUATING THE AUTHOR'S ARGUMENTS:

In this viewpoint, the author claims that marijuana may be safer than alcohol. What evidence and arguments does she use to support her statements? Based on this viewpoint alone, would you favor legalizing marijuana or not? Why or why not?

Viewpoint 2

Legal Marijuana Could Reduce Opioid Addiction

Richard Harris

"The findings suggest that expanding access to medical marijuana could help ease the opioid epidemic."

In the following viewpoint, the author explores how medical marijuana has affected use of opioids. Opioid drugs are powerful painkillers, which may be prescribed to treat moderate to severe pain. However, opioids can also be highly addictive. Overdoses, including death, are common. This viewpoint examines research of the number of opioid prescriptions in states with legal medical marijuana. In states where medical marijuana was easily available, fewer people got prescriptions for opioids. While legal medical marijuana is not likely to end the opioid addiction crisis, it may help. Richard Harris reports on science, medicine, and the environment for National Public Radio.

AS YOU READ, CONSIDER THE FOLLOWING QUESTIONS:
1. How can legal marijuana help people to use fewer opioid painkillers?
2. What risks are associated with using medical marijuana?
3. Why is it hard to study the effects of marijuana as a drug, according to the viewpoint?

Medical marijuana appears to have put a dent in the opioid abuse epidemic, according to two studies published Monday.

The research suggests that some people turn to marijuana as a way to treat their pain, and by so doing, avoid more dangerous addictive drugs. The findings are the latest to lend support to the idea that some people are willing to substitute marijuana for opioids and other prescription drugs.

Many people end up abusing opioid drugs such as oxycodone and heroin after starting off with a legitimate prescription for pain. The authors argue that people who avoid that first prescription are less likely to end up as part of the opioid epidemic.

"We do know that cannabis is much less risky than opiates, as far as likelihood of dependency," says W. David Bradford, a professor of public policy at the University of Georgia. "And certainly there's no mortality risk" from the drug itself.

The National Academies of Sciences, Engineering and Medicine says there's good evidence that cannabis is effective at treating pain for some conditions. So Bradford and three colleagues—including his scientist daughter—decided to see whether people who can get easy access to medical marijuana are less likely to get prescription opioids. The answer, they report in *JAMA Internal Medicine*, is yes.

"There are substantial reductions in opiate use" in states that have initiated dispensaries for medical marijuana, he says.

The researchers studied data from Medicare, which mostly covers people over the age of 65. (It was a convenient set of data and available to them at no cost.) They found a 14 percent reduction in opioid prescriptions in states that allow easy access to medical marijuana.

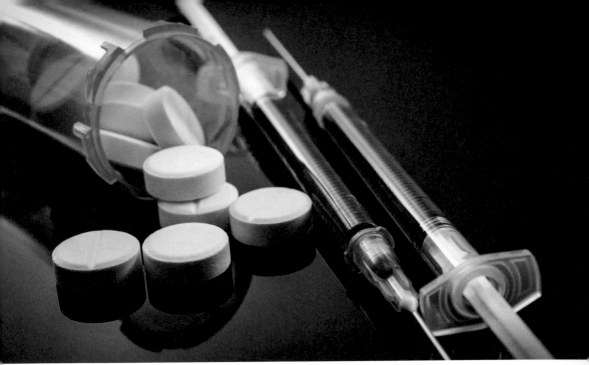

Opiates can be obtained legally by prescription or through the illegal drug market. They can be consumed as pills or injected. They tend to be highly addictive with prolonged use.

They estimate that these dispensary programs reduced the number of opioid prescriptions by 3.7 million daily doses. States that allowed homegrown marijuana for medical use saw an estimated 1.8 million fewer pills dispensed per day. To put that in perspective, from 2010 to 2015 Medicare recipients received an average of 23 million daily doses of opioids, the researchers say.

Because opioid use nationwide was rising during the study period, their estimate of reduced uses reflects a slowing of the increase, rather than an actual decline in opioid use in these states, Bradford says.

The analysis found a correlation and can't prove that marijuana use led to a reduction in the growth of opioid use. There might be other factors at work.

Even so, the findings suggest that expanding access to medical marijuana could help ease the opioid epidemic.

Hefei Wen at the University of Kentucky College of Public Health was lead author on another study in the same journal that reached similar conclusions. Wen, with Jason Hockenberry at Emory University, used Medicaid data. Medicaid is primarily a health insurance program for low-income people.

The authors write that laws that permit both medical marijuana and recreational marijuana for adults "have the potential to reduce opioid prescribing for Medicaid enrollees, a segment of population with disproportionately high risk for chronic pain, opioid use disorder and opioid overdose. Nevertheless, marijuana liberalization alone cannot solve the opioid epidemic."

Bradford agrees that medical marijuana laws could have a role to play. "But it is not without risks," he says. "Like any drug in our FDA-approved pharmacopeia, it can be misused. There's no question about it. So I hope nobody reading our study will say 'Oh, great, the answer to the opiate problem is just put cannabis in everybody's medicine chest and we are good to go.' We are certainly not saying that."

One concern is marijuana use might encourage people to experiment with more dangerous drugs. Dr. Mark Olfson, a professor of psychiatry and epidemiology at Columbia University, authored a study that found marijuana users were six times more likely than nonusers to abuse opioids.

"A young person starting marijuana is maybe putting him—or herself at increased risk," Olfson says. "On the other hand there may be a role—and there likely is a role—for medical marijuana in reducing the use of prescribed opioids for the management of pain."

This is a question of balancing risks and benefits. And that's difficult to do with the current studies based on broad populations—and in this case, populations that are not representative of the at-risk population as a whole.

Olfson says what they really need is studies that follow individuals, to see whether marijuana use really does supplant opioids. It's hard to do a study in this area because the federal government regards marijuana as a very dangerous drug and puts tight controls on research.

"That does make this a difficult area to study, and

that's unfortunate because we have a large problem with the opioid epidemic," Olfson says. "And at the same time, with an aging population, we have lots of people who have pain conditions and who will benefit from appropriate management."

EVALUATING THE AUTHOR'S ARGUMENTS:

In this viewpoint, the author quotes scientists who studied medical marijuana. How certain do they seem about their conclusions, and what contributed to this degree of certainty? What actions would you suggest that lawmakers take based on those conclusions?

Laws Against Marijuana Are Unfair and Ineffective

"People arrested for marijuana use pay heavy costs—and so may their families and associates."

Katherine Beckett

In the following viewpoint, the author explores how marijuana has affected the US justice system. She notes that a large percentage of drug arrests are for the possession of marijuana. Harsh penalties are imposed in an attempt to reduce drug use. Yet illegal marijuana has simply become more available. The author claims that enforcement efforts are expensive, and the money might be better spent in other ways. In addition, laws are not consistently enforced. They vary between states, and African Americans are more likely to be arrested and jailed. These biases can cause people to lose faith in the law. Katherine Beckett is a professor of sociology at the University of Washington. Her research focuses on the US criminal justice system.

AS YOU READ, CONSIDER THE FOLLOWING QUESTIONS:

1. Why are the penalties for possessing marijuana so serious?
2. Have laws against marijuana been successful in reducing its use?
3. What costs can someone face if arrested for marijuana possession?

"The Futility and High Cost of Criminalizing Marijuana," by Katherine Beckett, Scholars Strategy Network, December 1, 2012. Reprinted by permission.

Across the United States, tens of millions of residents have been arrested for violating marijuana laws. Arrests for offenses related to marijuana have increased dramatically since 1992. In 2010 alone, there were 853,838 arrests. Remarkably, more than half of all drug-related arrests that year involved marijuana alone. And almost nine of every ten people apprehended for marijuana offenses are charged with mere possession, not sales or distribution.

America's efforts to reduce marijuana use over the past four decades have largely depended on arrest, imprisonment, incarceration—and, recently, the seizure of private property through asset forfeiture laws. The aim of such heavy legal firepower is to deter potential consumers, reduce marijuana use, limit availability, and increase the price of the drug. But existing research suggests that these goals have not been achieved. Instead, prices have declined and increasingly potent marijuana has become more readily available to growing numbers of users—even as arrests have climbed. Developments are not the same in all states and localities, but overall there is no clear indication that intensified enforcement decreases marijuana use.

Marijuana Prohibition Is Costly for Society, Families and Individuals

Enforcement efforts against marijuana use may not work well, but they are still costly to the public as well as to the individuals and families involved.

- The savings that would follow from decriminalizing marijuana use are hard to calculate, but it is clear that the enforcement of marijuana laws consumes significant fiscal and organizational resources that could be allocated toward other public safety goals, or toward the provision of much-needed social services.
- The fiscal costs of marijuana enforcement are only partially offset by legal seizures of assets from convicted dealers. But the very possibility of asset forfeiture creates perverse incentives for police agencies and may reduce public safety.
- The enforcement of laws against simple use of marijuana creates additional pathologies in the criminal justice system—including

Almost nine out of ten marijuana-related arrests are for possession rather than distribution of the drug.

controversial policing tactics, the erosion of civil liberties, over-crowding in the courts, and the diversion of drug treatment dollars that could better be used to help more troubled offenders. The last problem appears when recreational marijuana smokers are required to participate in mandatory drug treatment programs.

- People arrested for marijuana use pay heavy costs—and so may their families and associates. Whether or not they are ultimately convicted, those arrested commonly incur lawyers' fees, fines and other court charges, and many also lose income and valuable assets. For both people apprehended and their families, arrests mean emotional stress and perhaps also the loss of faith in the fairness of the criminal justice process.
- Marijuana prohibition contributes to racial inequalities in the United States, because marijuana arrests are not evenly distributed across the population. Approximately 30% of those arrested for violating marijuana laws are African Americans, who pay the highest costs along with their families and communities.

Penalties and Enforcement Vary

The legal consequences of marijuana violations can be severe. But they are also uneven to the point of capriciousness, because laws and enforcement efforts are highly variable.

A number of US states have passed laws that permit the use of marijuana for medical purposes. Many municipalities have reduced the priority of enforcement. Some states have decriminalized marijuana altogether, while other jurisdictions mandate treatment for non-violent drug offenders rather than tossing them in prison.

The consequences for people convicted for marijuana offenses are also extremely variable. In states that have decriminalized marijuana, a person found in possession of the drug faces only a civil fine. In sharp contrast, in the state of Louisiana a person convicted the third time for possession of just one ounce of marijuana may be sentenced to twenty years in prison.

Can We Decriminalize Marijuana?

Researchers have used two main strategies to assess the impact of decriminalizing marijuana. One strategy compares patterns of marijuana use in jurisdictions with very different laws or enforcement policies. Another approach tracks shifts within jurisdictions where laws or enforcement practices have clearly changed. Both kinds of studies indicate that legal prohibitions and tough enforcement have little impact on rates of marijuana consumption. People use the drug regardless of whether they may face severe legal consequences.

In November 2012, majorities of citizens in Colorado and the state of Washington voted to make it made it legal to possess and smoke pot recreationally. When the new laws are certified, people

21 years and older will legally be able to possess up to an ounce of marijuana. In Colorado, people will also be able to grow as many as six plants; and in Washington, they will be able to obtain marijuana from state-licensed providers.

But these fledgling state laws conflict with federal drug policy. Marijuana is currently prohibited by the US government, classified as a "Schedule I controlled substance" with high potential for abuse and no safe or accepted medical use.

How will national authorities respond to the new legal directions charted by the voters of Colorado and Washington? The answers will become evident in coming months—and will have a big impact on the ability of all US states to adopt alternative and potentially more socially constructive approaches to the use and regulation of marijuana.

EVALUATING THE AUTHOR'S ARGUMENTS:

In this viewpoint, the author suggests that marijuana laws arc unfair. Is this a reason to make marijuana legal, or should the problem be addressed in a different way? Why do you think this? What are some other ways to address to the problem?

Legal Marijuana Brings In Tax Money

Gavin Ekins and Joseph Bishop-Henchman

"In those states that have fully legalized marijuana, revenue collections have exceeded initial estimates."

In the following viewpoint, tax experts address how legal marijuana has affected taxes. They note that states where marijuana is legal have already seen a substantial increase in tax income. They suggest that making marijuana legal nationwide could further increase tax income at the federal, state, and local levels. Not only would marijuana bring in sales tax money, but industry workers would also pay taxes on their wages. If marijuana were made legal at the federal level, it would have several tax effects. Over time, tax income should stabilize, and the authors attempt to predict how this might play out. Joe Bishop-Henchman is Executive Vice President at the Tax Foundation, where Gavin Ekins is a research economist. The Tax Foundation is a nonprofit agency that conducts research and analysis on tax policy.

"Marijuana Legalization and Taxes: Federal Revenue Impact," by Gavin Ekins and Joseph Bishop-Henchman, Tax Foundation, March 12, 2016. Reprinted by permission.

1. How much tax revenue could be earned on marijuana if all states made it legal?
2. What kind of taxes can marijuana sales provide?
3. How would nationwide legalization likely affect taxes from marijuana sales?

Four states and the District of Columbia have legalized the sale of retail marijuana by popular vote, with an additional 25 states permitting medical marijuana or decriminalizing marijuana possession. Beginning in 2011, polls consistently show a majority of Americans supportive of legalizing marijuana, and a number of states are likely to consider legalization ballot initiatives or legislative measures in the next few years.

In those states that have fully legalized marijuana, revenue collections have exceeded initial estimates. Colorado anticipated $70 million in marijuana tax collections per year, and after a slow initial start, state collections will likely exceed $140 million in calendar year 2016. In Washington, after a slow start to bring the licensing system online, sales are now averaging over $2 million a day with revenue possibly reaching $270 million per year. If all states legalized and taxed marijuana, states could collectively expect to raise between $5 billion and $18 billion per year. While these amounts are not stratospheric, they are considerable and exceed additional enforcement and regulatory costs incurred by the states.

Estimated Revenue Impact of Legal Marijuana

It is estimated that the current size of the marijuana market nationally is $45 billion per year, approximately 0.28 percent of gross domestic product and comprising some 26 million pounds of marijuana consumed per year.

Federal and state governments have several options for taxes on a legal marijuana industry. A federal excise tax on marijuana similar to that of cigarettes, approximately $23 per pound of product, would raise approximately $500 million in additional revenue. A 10 percent

Marijuana that is legally sold in a dispensary could be taxed like other goods, which would provide federal and state tax revenue.

sales surtax, similar in nature to those adopted recently by Colorado and other states and proposed in recent legislation by Rep. Earl Blumenauer, would raise approximately $5.3 billion in additional revenue; higher excise tax rates would raise proportionately more.

Business income from marijuana production would initially raise almost $5.5 billion in federal revenues and an additional $1.5 billion in state and local revenues. These revenues are expected to fall as more businesses enter into the market and drive down profit margins. Individual income tax and payroll taxes from labor in the marijuana industry, which would be reported after legalization, contributes $1.5 billion in federal revenue and an additional $1 billion in state and local revenues. These revenues are expected to increase as production expands.

At the state level, assuming no black market, state taxes on marijuana similar to Washington and Colorado could increase state's tax revenues by $13 billion nationally, with an additional $5 billion from normal sales taxes. If high tax rates or other factors perpetuate the black market, tax collections would be less.

Effect of Legalization on the Marijuana Market

Two economic forces will act on the marijuana market when recreational use is legalized. First, those currently involved in the marijuana trade require a higher return than the rest of the economy due to the high risk of imprisonment, confiscation of capital, and unenforceable contracts. Anecdotal estimates suggests that profit margins need to be 100 percent and can be as high as 1000 percent. This is considerably higher than profit margins of similar industries, such as the tobacco industry. Legalizing marijuana will drastically reduce the risk involved in producing marijuana, which reduces the required return to engage in the activity. The lower risk should increase the entrance of new entrepreneurs into the market, which increases supply and forces down prices.

The second force is the inclusion of taxes in the price. Taxes, which are not levied directly in the black market, should have an upward pressure on prices. Many taxes are passed directly to the consumer through higher prices. Marijuana, similar to alcohol and tobacco products, is less sensitive to changes in price than other products. Thus, a tax increase is likely to be passed directly to the consumer. At the same time, when businesses operate in the black market, there is a considerable loss of tax revenue to federal, state, and local governments. These losses are not solely from sales and excise taxes. Business, wage income, and payroll taxes as well as business and licensing fees are also lost.

Using estimates of demand, from domestic and international studies, and the long-run after-tax profit margins from the alcohol and tobacco industries, we estimate that overall taxes should fall from over $28 billion to just over $22 billion, assuming that all states implement a 25 percent sales surtax and the federal government has an excise tax similar to that of cigarette. The change in tax revenues is largely from a reduction in business profits as production increases and profit margins fall. In addition, as the price of marijuana falls due to increased production, sales tax revenues should also decrease somewhat.

EVALUATING THE AUTHOR'S ARGUMENTS:

In this viewpoint, the authors suggest that making marijuana legal would increase tax revenues. Is that alone a reason to make something illegal? What other factors should be considered? What costs could legal marijuana have for the country?

We Can't Prove That Marijuana Is a Gateway Drug

Dave Levitan

"Though there are correlations between marijuana use and other drugs, there is no conclusive evidence that one actually causes the other."

In the following viewpoint, the author debates whether marijuana is a gateway drug. A drug could be a gateway if it changes the brain in ways that make the user more likely to abuse other drugs. Some studies suggest that youth who use marijuana, alcohol, or nicotine could undergo such changes. A drug could also be a gateway for cultural or social reasons. For example, people who are around marijuana users may be more likely to try a variety of drugs. Individuals may also engage in risk-taking behavior, which could include the use of marijuana and other drugs. It does appear that people who use marijuana are later more likely to use other drugs. However, that does not mean marijuana use causes people to use other drugs. Overall, the question is still under debate among the scientific community. Dave Levitan was a science writer at FactCheck.org.

AS YOU READ, CONSIDER THE FOLLOWING QUESTIONS:
  1. What is meant by a gateway drug?
  2. Does research indicate that marijuana use leads to later use of illegal drugs?
  3. What other factors may contribute to drug abuse?

C hris Christie said that marijuana is a "gateway drug" while arguing for enforcement of its federal status as an illegal substance. Though there are correlations between marijuana use and other drugs, there is no conclusive evidence that one actually causes the other. The science on this topic is far from settled.

In an interview on Hugh Hewitt's radio show on April 14, Christie, the governor of New Jersey and a potential 2016 presidential candidate, said he would crack down on marijuana sales and use in Washington and Colorado, which in 2012 were the first two states to legalize marijuana for recreational use. "Marijuana is a gateway drug," Christie said. "We have an enormous addiction problem in this country."

The "gateway hypothesis" or theory refers to the idea that one substance—marijuana, in this case—leads users to subsequently use and/or abuse other drugs. If Christie's point is simply that the use of marijuana tends to precede the use of other drugs, then he is correct—but that's not the whole story.

Though studies of large populations of people have indeed found that those who smoke marijuana are more likely to use other drugs, these studies show a correlation without showing causation—a commonly misunderstood phenomenon in science. In short, just because marijuana smokers might be more likely to later use, say, cocaine, does not imply that using marijuana causes one to use cocaine.

A 1999 report from the Institute of Medicine, which is part of the National Academy of Sciences, laid out this issue clearly (see pages 100–101): "In the sense that marijuana use typically precedes rather than follows initiation into the use of other illicit drugs, it is indeed a gateway drug. However, it does not appear to be a gateway drug to the extent that it is the *cause* or even that it is the most significant predictor of serious drug abuse; that is, care must be taken not to attribute cause to association."

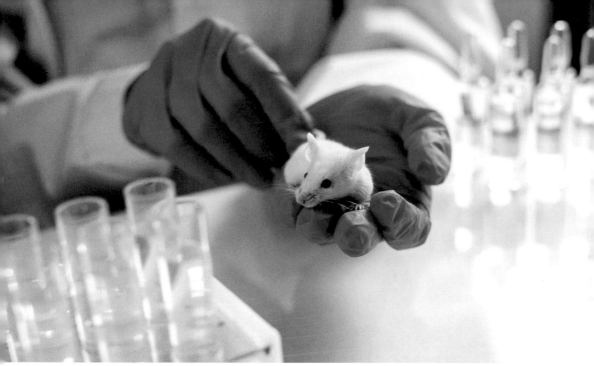

Lab tests with rats suggest that THC could impact the development of an adolescent's brain if used at a young age.

We spoke with several experts and reviewed the available scientific literature on gateway theory. Christie's definitive statement is unsupported by evidence—there is some evidence in favor of a gateway effect, but the scientific community shares no consensus on the issue and there is little evidence on the underlying cause of that effect.

Biological Mechanisms

Importantly, there are two distinct ways in which marijuana or other drugs might act as a gateway: biological or pharmacological reasons why marijuana would lead to other drugs (sometimes known as the "stepping stone" theory); and social or cultural reasons for the jump from one drug to another. In the case of the first idea, some research has found plausible biological ways in which marijuana—and, notably, nicotine and alcohol—could "prime" the brain and make one more likely to abuse other drugs, but this research is largely in rats and is not conclusive.

"There are some studies that have been done in animals and they suggest that there may be changes that marijuana produces in the brain that can be long lasting when the animal is exposed to it as an adolescent," said Susan Weiss, the associate director for scientific affairs at the National Institute on Drug Abuse, which is part of the National Institutes of Health, in a phone call.

For example, in one study published in 2007 in the journal *Neuropsychopharmacology*, researchers treated some adolescent rats with THC, the main active compound in marijuana. The rats were then given the opportunity to "self-administer" heroin as adults. The THC-treated rats consistently increased their heroin usage, while those rats that had not been treated with THC maintained a steady level of heroin intake.

Another study, published in 2014 in *European Neuropsychopharmacology*, similarly found that adolescent THC exposure in rats seemed to change the rodents' brains. The rats treated with THC exhibited more anxiety-like behaviors, and also exhibited more "heroin-seeking" behavior later in life. The authors concluded that, at least in rats, chronic exposure to THC during adolescence could indeed be responsible for "increased vulnerability to drug relapse in adulthood." Another rat study, from *Biological Psychiatry* in 2004, also found that THC exposure induced "cross-tolerance" that could increase later usage of cocaine, morphine, and amphetamine.

Notably though, these findings are not unique to marijuana. Weiss told us that nicotine and alcohol, two other drugs that are widely available to young people and are often among the first drugs used, have been found to have similar effects in animal studies. One such study, published in the journal *Science Translational Medicine* in 2011, showed that treating mice with nicotine induced genetic changes that increased the response to cocaine. Interestingly, this only worked in one direction, when the mice were treated with nicotine and then co-treated with both nicotine and cocaine; if cocaine was administered first, the effect was not seen, suggesting there may be a gateway effect from nicotine to cocaine.

The studies on brain chemistry and the influence of marijuana on responses to other drugs only has taken place in those animal studies, meaning extrapolation to humans is problematic. We do have some hints of biological gateway effects in humans, though, from studies involving twins.

One such study, which was published in the *Journal of the American Medical Association* in 2003, and involved 311 twin pairs "discordant" for early marijuana use—that is, one of each set of twins had used marijuana before the age of 17, and the other had not. The twin that did use marijuana early in life had between a 2.1- and 5.2-times higher risk of other drug use, alcohol dependence, and drug abuse/dependence than their sibling. This means that associations between marijuana use and later drug use can't be explained by genetic factors, and gives support to the gateway theory.

But even this leaves a lot of unanswered questions, according to Weiss. "Did marijuana change that twin and make them more likely to use other drugs? What was it about that one twin that made them use marijuana while the other twin didn't? We don't know the answer to that. Did he happen to have friends that were more deviant? It's very difficult to completely interpret these things; most likely there is probably some convergence of factors."

And indeed, a subsequent twin study published in *Development and Psychopathology* in 2008 called the results of the first into question. The paper found a similar difference between twins with regard to early marijuana use and later drug use, but only in non-identical twins. To the authors, this supported the idea that there are too many factors to conclude in one direction or the other: "[T]he longitudinal pattern of drug use that has been interpreted as the 'gateway effect' might be better conceptualized as a genetically influenced developmental trajectory."

Hidden Causes and International Patterns

Clearly, the biological evidence for a gateway effect is varied and difficult to interpret. Unfortunately, specific evidence for the other possible mechanisms are also far from clear and definitive.

The cultural and social version of the gateway theory posits that simply by being around marijuana and the people who use it one might be more likely to end up trying and using other drugs as well. There is also the idea that an individual who uses marijuana habitually may simply be more likely to engage in risk-taking behavior, and thus will seek out the other drugs. This would suggest there is no causal link from marijuana to other drugs, it is only a function of marijuana's

A relationship between two or more variables is called association or correlation. A positive correlation means that when one variable goes up, so does the other. A negative correlation means that when one variable goes up, another goes down. Correlation only means there appears to be a relationship, but does not prove cause and effect.

general availability versus other more difficult-to-obtain substances.

Some researchers, though, think there is almost certainly a causal link—it's just not clear what it is. David Fergusson is a professor at the University of Otago in Christchurch, New Zealand, and he has been leading the Christchurch Health and Development Study, a 35-year, ongoing look at 1,265 New Zealanders born in 1977. Several papers on drug use and the gateway effect have emerged from this study.

"There is a very strong association between the use of cannabis in adolescence and subsequent use of other illicit drugs," Fergusson told us in an email. He said that one analysis from his study published in the journal *Addiction* used a statistical test that "clearly suggest the existence of some kind of causative association in which the use of cannabis increases the likelihood that the user will go on to use other illicit drugs ... Where things get murky is in the area of the nature of the causal processes."

Another possible contributor to those processes is simply the availability of a given drug that might lead it to be used first, rather than any particular biological reason for moving from one to another. A large international collaboration produced a study published in the journal *Drug and Alcohol Dependence* in 2010 that looked at patterns of drug use across 17 countries. The study found that "[w]ith few exceptions, substances earlier in the 'gateway' sequence predicted drug use later in the sequence." That finding, though, differed in strength across countries.

Those early-sequence drugs included marijuana, alcohol, or nicotine. Different countries had different patterns of drug use in general, and also different patterns of gateway "violations"—that is, when people used other illicit drugs without ever trying those early drugs.

For example, Japan had very low rates of marijuana use (1.6 percent by age 29), and also had more people use other illicit drugs before the early-use drugs than in other countries. The authors wrote, "a lack of exposure and/or access to substances earlier in the normative sequence did not correspond to reductions in overall levels of other illicit drug use." In other words: limiting access to marijuana might not have any effect on heroin and cocaine use.

That study also provides a hint that marijuana's illegal status may contribute to its gateway effects. The mechanism here is simple: accessing one illegal drug simply means a marijuana user would be more likely to have access to other illegal drugs, through social interactions and the act of actually buying the drug. The *Drug and Alcohol Dependence* study found that marijuana use was less strongly associated with other illicit drug use in the Netherlands, where marijuana can legally be purchased in so-called coffee shops, than in other countries including the United States.

A working report from the Rand Drug Policy Research Center looked at the Dutch experience with legalized marijuana as well. According to that paper, the US actually has slightly higher rates of use than the Netherlands, and there is evidence for a "weakened gateway" in the Netherlands: about 15 of every 100 cannabis users have tried cocaine in that country, a lower rate than others where marijuana is illegal such as Scotland, Italy, and Norway. The same is true for amphetamine use.

Fergusson told us that more research is still needed to truly understand what the causal link between marijuana and other drugs might be. "It is my view that when the jury comes in, what will be found is a complex multivariate situation in which the greater susceptibility of cannabis to illicit drug use is the end point of a complex mix of factors including: the neurophysiological effects of cannabis; social and peer influences; and the legal status of cannabis," he said.

Weiss, of NIDA, said that scientifically a gateway effect cannot be ruled out, but a conclusive "yes" is also not possible at this point. "The scientific community is still arguing about it," she told us. "It really is a complicated thing to tease out. It has been very contentious over the years. And I don't know how useful it is as a concept, but it's something that people latch on to."

Christie is entitled to his opinions on the legality of marijuana and the statutes in Washington and Colorado, and he is right that marijuana use "typically precedes" the use of other illegal drugs, as the Institute of Medicine report said. But there is no firm ground to stand on when making claims of the drug's gateway effect.

EVALUATING THE AUTHOR'S ARGUMENTS:

In this viewpoint, the author notes that marijuana may not be a gateway drug. However, there is an association between marijuana use and the use of other drugs. What are the benefits of knowing how marijuana use affects other drug use? Do you believe we have enough information yet to reach conclusions?

Chapter 2

Are There Dangers to Legalizing Marijuana?

The Drug Enforcement Administration (DEA) confiscates illegal cannabis plants.

Marijuana Use Has Many Risks

> *"When people begin using marijuana as teenagers, the drug may impair thinking, memory, and learning functions."*

National Institute on Drug Abuse

The following viewpoint explains what marijuana is and how it is typically used. It describes the short-term and long-term effects on the brain. Marijuana has several short-term effects, depending on the dosage. Over the long-term, marijuana can affect brain development. The viewpoint then addresses the physical effects of marijuana, including potential damage to the heart and lungs. It notes that long-term use has been linked to mental illness in some people. Secondhand marijuana smoke is unlikely to make someone very high, but more research is needed to know if secondhand marijuana smoke has health risks. According to this source, marijuana is addictive, and frequent users have less satisfaction in life. The National Institute on Drug Abuse is part of the US Department of Health and Human Services.

AS YOU READ, CONSIDER THE FOLLOWING QUESTIONS:
1. What is THC?
2. What are the effects of marijuana when taken in high doses?
3. How does marijuana use affect teens differently from adults?

"Marijuana," National Institute on Drug Abuse, June 2018.

Marijuana refers to the dried leaves, flowers, stems, and seeds from the *Cannabis sativa* or *Cannabis indica* plant. The plant contains the mind-altering chemical THC and other similar compounds. Extracts can also be made from the cannabis plant.

Marijuana is the most commonly used illicit drug in the United States.[1] Its use is widespread among young people. In 2015, more than 11 million young adults ages 18 to 25 used marijuana in the past year. According to the Monitoring the Future survey, rates of marijuana use among middle and high school students have dropped or leveled off in the past few years after several years of increase. However, the number of young people who believe regular marijuana use is risky is decreasing.

Legalization of marijuana for medical use or adult recreational use in a growing number of states may affect these views.

How Do People Use Marijuana?

People smoke marijuana in hand-rolled cigarettes (joints) or in pipes or water pipes (bongs). They also smoke it in blunts—emptied cigars that have been partly or completely refilled with marijuana. To avoid inhaling smoke, some people are using vaporizers. These devices pull the active ingredients (including THC) from the marijuana and collect their vapor in a storage unit. A person then inhales the vapor, not the smoke. Some vaporizers use a liquid marijuana extract.

People can mix marijuana in food (*edibles*), such as brownies, cookies, or candy, or brew it as a tea. A newly popular method of use is smoking or eating different forms of THC-rich resins.

Marijuana Extracts

Smoking THC-rich resins extracted from the marijuana plant is on the rise. People call this practice *dabbing*. These extracts come in various forms, such as:

- *hash oil* or *honey oil*—a gooey liquid
- *wax* or *budder*—a soft solid with a texture like lip balm
- *shatter*—a hard, amber-colored solid

THC and the brain

Tetrahydrocannabinol (THC), the psychoactive substance found in cannabis, affects the body when marijuana is smoked or otherwise ingested. Located throughout the body, cannabinoid receptors are found in greatest quantity in the brain, particularly in areas that govern coordination, judgment, learning and memory. Some of the areas THC affects:

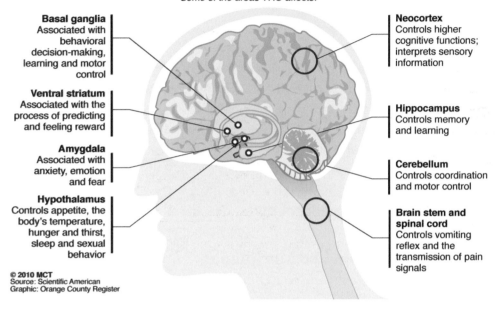

Basal ganglia
Associated with behavioral decision-making, learning and motor control

Ventral striatum
Associated with the process of predicting and feeling reward

Amygdala
Associated with anxiety, emotion and fear

Hypothalamus
Controls appetite, the body's temperature, hunger and thirst, sleep and sexual behavior

Neocortex
Controls higher cognitive functions; interprets sensory information

Hippocampus
Controls memory and learning

Cerebellum
Controls coordination and motor control

Brain stem and spinal cord
Controls vomiting reflex and the transmission of pain signals

© 2010 MCT
Source: Scientific American
Graphic: Orange County Register

The substance found in marijuana known as THC impacts various different parts of the brain, causing both long-term and short-term effects.

These extracts can deliver extremely large amounts of THC to the body, and their use has sent some people to the emergency room. Another danger is in preparing these extracts, which usually involves butane (lighter fluid). A number of people have caused fires and explosions and have been seriously burned from using butane to make extracts at home.

How Does Marijuana Affect the Brain?
Marijuana has both short-and long-term effects on the brain.

Short-Term Effects
When a person smokes marijuana, THC quickly passes from the lungs into the bloodstream. The blood carries the chemical to the brain and other organs throughout the body. The body absorbs THC

more slowly when the person eats or drinks it. In that case, they generally feel the effects after 30 minutes to 1 hour.

THC acts on specific brain cell receptors that ordinarily react to natural THC-like chemicals. These natural chemicals play a role in normal brain development and function.

Marijuana overactivates parts of the brain that contain the highest number of these receptors. This causes the "high" that people feel. Other effects include:

- altered senses (for example, seeing brighter colors)
- altered sense of time
- changes in mood
- impaired body movement
- difficulty with thinking and problem-solving
- impaired memory
- hallucinations (when taken in high doses)
- delusions (when taken in high doses)
- psychosis (when taken in high doses)

Long-Term Effects

Marijuana also affects brain development. When people begin using marijuana as teenagers, the drug may impair thinking, memory, and learning functions and affect how the brain builds connections between the areas necessary for these functions. Researchers are still studying how long marijuana's effects last and whether some changes may be permanent.

For example, a study from New Zealand conducted in part by researchers at Duke University showed that people who started smoking marijuana heavily in their teens and had an ongoing marijuana use disorder lost an average of 8 IQ points between ages 13 and 38. The lost mental abilities didn't fully return in those who quit marijuana as adults. Those who started smoking marijuana as adults didn't show notable IQ declines.

In another recent study on twins, those who used marijuana showed a significant decline in general knowledge and in verbal ability (equivalent to 4 IQ points) between the preteen years and early adulthood, but no predictable difference was found between twins when one used marijuana and the other didn't. This suggests that the IQ decline in marijuana users may be caused by something other than marijuana, such as shared familial factors (e.g., genetics, family environment). NIDA's Adolescent Brain Cognitive Development (ABCD) study, a major longitudinal study, is tracking a large sample of young Americans from late childhood to early adulthood to help clarify how and to what extent marijuana and other substances, alone and in combination, affect adolescent brain development.

A Rise in Marijuana's THC Levels

The amount of THC in marijuana has been increasing steadily over the past few decades. For a person who's new to marijuana use, this may mean exposure to higher THC levels with a greater chance of a harmful reaction. Higher THC levels may explain the rise in emergency room visits involving marijuana use.

The popularity of edibles also increases the chance of harmful reactions. Edibles take longer to digest and produce a high. Therefore, people may consume more to feel the effects faster, leading to dangerous results.

Higher THC levels may also mean a greater risk for addiction if people are regularly exposing themselves to high doses.

What Are the Other Health Effects of Marijuana?

Marijuana use may have a wide range of effects, both physical and mental.

Physical Effects

- Breathing problems. Marijuana smoke irritates the lungs, and people who smoke marijuana frequently can have the same breathing problems as those who smoke tobacco. These problems include daily cough and phlegm, more frequent lung illness, and a higher risk of lung infections. Researchers so far haven't found a higher risk for lung cancer in people who smoke marijuana.

- Increased heart rate. Marijuana raises heart rate for up to 3 hours after smoking. This effect may increase the chance of heart attack. Older people and those with heart problems may be at higher risk.
- Problems with child development during and after pregnancy. One study found that about 20% of pregnant women 24-years-old and younger screened positive for marijuana. However, this study also found that women were about twice as likely to screen positive for marijuana use via a drug test than they state in self-reported measures. This suggests that self-reported rates of marijuana use in pregnant females is not an accurate measure of marijuana use and may be underreporting their use. Additionally, in one study of dispensaries, nonmedical personnel at marijuana dispensaries were recommending marijuana to pregnant women for nausea, but medical experts warn against it. This concerns medical experts because marijuana use during pregnancy is linked to lower birth weight and increased risk of both brain and behavioral problems in babies. If a pregnant woman uses marijuana, the drug may affect certain developing parts of the fetus's brain. Children exposed to marijuana in the womb have an increased risk of problems with attention, memory, and problem-solving com-pared to unexposed children. Some research also suggests that moderate amounts of THC are excreted into the breast milk of nursing mothers. With regular use, THC can reach amounts in breast milk that could affect the baby's developing brain. More research is needed.
- Intense Nausea and Vomiting. Regular, long-term marijuana use can lead to some people to develop Cannabinoid Hyperemesis Syndrome. This causes users to experience regular cycles of severe nausea, vomiting, and dehydration, sometimes requiring emergency medical attention.

Mental Effects

Long-term marijuana use has been linked to mental illness in some people, such as:

- temporary hallucinations
- temporary paranoia
- worsening symptoms in patients with schizophrenia—a severe mental disorder with symptoms such as hallucinations, paranoia, and disorganized thinking

Marijuana use has also been linked to other mental health problems, such as depression, anxiety, and suicidal thoughts among teens. However, study findings have been mixed.

Are There Effects of Inhaling Secondhand Marijuana Smoke?

Failing a Drug Test?

While it's possible to fail a drug test after inhaling secondhand marijuana smoke, it's unlikely. Studies show that very little THC is released in the air when a person exhales. Research findings suggest that, unless people are in an enclosed room, breathing in lots of smoke for hours at close range, they aren't likely to fail a drug test. Even if some THC was found in the blood, it wouldn't be enough to fail a test.

Getting High from Passive Exposure?

Similarly, it's unlikely that secondhand marijuana smoke would give nonsmoking people in a confined space a high from passive exposure. Studies have shown that people who don't use marijuana report only mild effects of the drug from a nearby smoker, under extreme conditions (breathing in lots of marijuana smoke for hours in an enclosed room).

Other Health Effects?

More research is needed to know if secondhand marijuana smoke has similar health risks as secondhand tobacco smoke. A recent study on rats suggests that secondhand marijuana smoke can do as much damage to the heart and blood vessels as secondhand tobacco smoke.

But researchers haven't fully explored the effect of secondhand marijuana smoke on humans. What they do know is that the toxins and tar found in marijuana smoke could affect vulnerable people, such as children or people with asthma.

How Does Marijuana Affect a Person's Life?

Compared to those who don't use marijuana, those who frequently use large amounts report the following:

- lower life satisfaction
- poorer mental health
- poorer physical health
- more relationship problems

People also report less academic and career success. For example, marijuana use is linked to a higher likelihood of dropping out of school. It's also linked to more job absences, accidents, and injuries.

Is Marijuana a Gateway Drug?

Use of alcohol, tobacco, and marijuana are likely to come before use of other drugs. Animal studies have shown that early exposure to addictive substances, including THC, may change how the brain responds to other drugs. For example, when rodents are repeatedly exposed to THC when they're young, they later show an enhanced response to other addictive substances—such as morphine or nicotine—in the areas of the brain that control reward, and they're more likely to show addiction-like behaviors.

Although these findings support the idea of marijuana as a "gateway drug," the majority of people who use marijuana don't go on to use other "harder" drugs. It's also important to note that other factors besides biological mechanisms, such as a person's social environment, are also critical in a person's risk for drug use and addiction.

Can a Person Overdose on Marijuana?

An overdose occurs when a person uses enough of the drug to produce life-threatening symptoms or death. There are no reports of teens or adults dying from marijuana alone. However, some people who use marijuana can feel some very uncomfortable side effects, especially when using marijuana products with high THC levels. People have reported symptoms such as anxiety and paranoia, and in rare cases, an extreme psychotic reaction (which can include delusions and hallucinations) that can lead them to seek treatment in an emergency room.

While a psychotic reaction can occur following any method of use, emergency room responders have seen an increasing number of cases involving marijuana edibles. Some people (especially preteens and teens) who know very little about edibles don't realize that it takes longer for the body to feel marijuana's effects when eaten rather than smoked. So they consume more of the edible, trying to get high faster or thinking they haven't taken enough. In addition, some babies and toddlers have been seriously ill after ingesting marijuana or marijuana edibles left around the house.

Is Marijuana Addictive?

Marijuana use can lead to the development of a substance use disorder, a medical illness in which the person is unable to stop using even though it's causing health and social problems in their life. Severe substance use disorders are also known as addiction. Research suggests that between 9 and 30 percent of those who use marijuana may develop some degree of marijuana use disorder. People who begin using marijuana before age 18 are four to seven times more likely than adults to develop a marijuana use disorder.

Many people who use marijuana long term and are trying to quit report mild withdrawal symptoms that make quitting difficult. These include:

- grouchiness
- sleeplessness
- decreased appetite
- anxiety
- cravings

What Treatments Are Available for Marijuana Use Disorder?

No medications are currently available to treat marijuana use disorder, but behavioral support has been shown to be effective. Examples include therapy and motivational incentives (providing rewards to patients who remain drug-free). Continuing research may lead to new medications that help ease withdrawal symptoms, block the effects of marijuana, and prevent relapse.

EVALUATING THE AUTHOR'S ARGUMENTS:

Look over the viewpoint closely. Does it appear biased or unbiased? What led you to your conclusions? This viewpoint is from a US government department. How does that affect your confidence in the information provided?

Marijuana Causes Accidents and Death

"Given the amount of evidence— both scientific and anecdotal— there simply does not seem to be any way around it: Marijuana is responsible for many deaths."

Jerry Cox

In the following viewpoint, the author refutes the idea that no one has died from marijuana use. He suggests many deaths can be attributed to marijuana. Drivers high on marijuana can cause vehicular accidents. It may contribute to suicide or murder. A few deaths have even been directly blamed on marijuana. In addition, people can suffer after unknowingly consuming marijuana products, and children and teenagers are the most common victims of accidental overdoses. Jerry Cox is the founder and president of Arkansas Family Council, which is intended to promote traditional family values and support public policy that helps to protect them.

AS YOU READ, CONSIDER THE FOLLOWING QUESTIONS:
1. How much does marijuana use contribute to vehicular accidents?
2. How can marijuana cause explosions?
3. How can children be accidentally harmed by marijuana?

"Number of Deaths Caused by Marijuana Much More than 0," by Jerry Cox, Arkansas Family Council, March 19, 2015. Reprinted by permission.

F rom time-to-time proponents of marijuana legalization throw out some fuzzy statistics claiming no one has ever died from marijuana.

Case-in-point, earlier this month a group in Arkansas advocating major changes in our state's marijuana laws tweeted the following:

> **@ARDPEG**
> *Alcohol kills 88,000/year in the US It's not even a medicine. No one has died from cannabis—ever. @TomCottonAR #GetEducated #arpx #arnews*

"No one has ever died from cannabis." Let's investigate this claim.

Unpacking the Statistics on Alcohol and Marijuana

In the tweet above, Arkansans for Compassionate Care is apparently citing a statistic from the Centers for Disease Control on the number of deaths from alcohol every year (88,000, on average). If we read how the CDC arrived at that figure, we see it was by calculating the number of alcohol-related accidents and health problems.

In other words, it isn't simply that 88,000 people die from blood alcohol poisoning (which some might describe as an "alcohol over-dose") each year. Alcohol is contributing to the deaths of about 88,000 people each year in the form of heart and liver problems, car crashes, and so on.

These are what the CDC calls "alcohol attributable deaths." They are deaths cause by something that was a direct effect of alcohol use.

So let's take a look at marijuana-attributable deaths. Has marijuana really never killed anyone, as so many of its proponents claim?

Kevin Sabet with Smart Approaches to Marijuana did an interview with *The Daily Signal* last year in which he took the claim to task, saying,

> *"Saying marijuana … has never killed anyone is like saying tobacco has never killed anyone. Nobody dies from a tobacco overdose. You can't smoke yourself to death. And yet nobody would dispute that tobacco causes death … You die from lung cancer—you don't die from smoking. You die from what smoking did to your lungs, which is a direct effect*

from smoking. And so in that same way marijuana does kill people in the form of mental illnesses and suicide, in the form of car crashes ... You can't say marijuana doesn't kill."

Marijuana-Attributable Deaths

A little research reveals news articles, police reports, and academic studies on a number of marijuana-attributable deaths:

1. December, 2014: The National Institute on Drug Abuse updated its marijuana research paper, saying, "Marijuana is the illicit drug most frequently found in the blood of drivers who have been involved in accidents, including fatal ones," and citing research that marijuana is increasingly detected in fatal vehicle accidents.

2. December, 2014: Oklahoma authorities reported a man with marijuana both in his system and on his person drove into oncoming traffic, crashing into another vehicle and killing its driver.

3. May, 2014: A study published by the University of Colorado School of Medicine found that, "the proportion of marijuana-positive drivers involved in fatal motor vehicle crashes in Colorado has increased dramatically since the commercialization of medical marijuana in the middle of 2009."

4. April, 2014: A 47-year-old Denver man allegedly shot his wife while she spoke with a 911 dispatcher over the phone. According to various reports, the wife called 911 after her husband consumed candy laced with marijuana and began hallucinating and frightening the couple's children. Some sources indicate the man may have taken prescription drugs with the marijuana. CBS News reports that 12 minutes into the call with 911, the wife "told dispatchers her husband was getting a gun from a safe before a gunshot sounded and the line went quiet." The marijuana candy had, apparently, been purchased [at] a licensed shop in the Denver area.

5. April, 2014: Researchers writing in the *Journal of the American Heart Association* investigated marijuana's effects on cardiovascular health. They reviewed 1,979 incidents from 2006 to 2011, and found, "there were 22 cardiac complications (20

acute coronary syndromes), 10 peripheral complications (lower limb or juvenile arteriopathies and Buerger-like diseases), and 3 cerebral complications (acute cerebral angiopathy, transient cortical blindness, and spasm of cerebral artery). In 9 cases, the event led to patient death." (Emphasis added).

6. March, 2014: A 19-year-old college student jumped to his death after eating a marijuana-laced cookie purchased at a licensed marijuana store in Colorado. Reports indicate the man began shaking, screaming, and throwing objects in his hotel room after eating the marijuana "edible." He ultimately jumped over the fourth-floor railing, into the lobby of the hotel at which he was staying. According to CBS News, the autopsy report listed marijuana as a "significant contributing factor" to his death.

7. February, 2014: researchers from Germany determined the deaths of two apparently-healthy, young men were in fact the result of marijuana According to their article published in the journal *Forensic Science International*. Researchers concluded, "After exclusion of other causes of death, we assume that the young men died from cardiovascular complications evoked by smoking cannabis."

8. November, 2013: Seattle news outlets reported an elderly Washington resident was killed after a neighbor's apartment exploded as a result of a hash oil operation. Hash oil is a highly-potent extract produced from marijuana using flammable chemicals such as butane.

9. June, 2013: A 35-year-old Oregon man died as a result of an explosion and fire caused by a hash oil operation he and a friend were conducting in a garage.

10. October, 2011: The Office of National Drug Control Policy released a report analyzing traffic accidents from 2005–2009. The report noted, "Among fatally injured males who tested positive for drugs, 28 percent tested positive for cannabinoids compared with 17 percent of females," and that, "Cannabinoids were reported in 43 percent of fatally injured drivers under age 24 who tested positive for drugs."

11. 2004: A study in the official journal of the American Academy of Pediatrics examined case studies of three otherwise-healthy

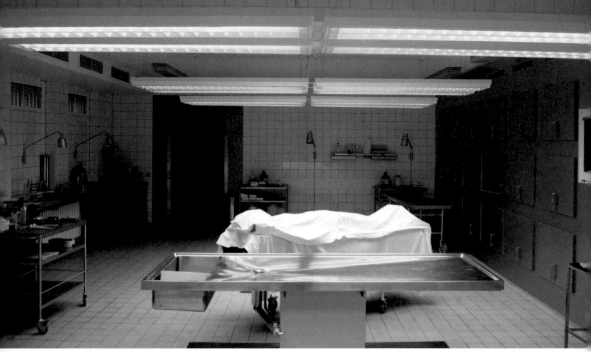

While simply using marijuana is unlikely to cause an overdose death, when combined with other health and lifestyle factors it can have a fatal impact.

adolescent boys who were admitted to hospitals due to stroke following heavy marijuana use; two of the boys ultimately died, and the study concluded marijuana may cause stroke and death.

These are just a few reports on deaths linked to marijuana. According to well-publicized FOIA responses, from 1997 to 2005 the FDA recorded 279 marijuana-related deaths—long before Colorado voters decided to legalize the drug.

We have brought up many of these statistics before in our discussions on marijuana. Each time we did, marijuana supporters tried to evade by arguing that marijuana hasn't caused as many deaths as other drugs. However, there is a world of difference between claiming marijuana has never killed a single person and claiming marijuana has not killed as many people as other substances.

Emergencies Caused by Marijuana

Besides death, marijuana has caused or contributed to many well-documented emergencies. Some of these emergencies easily could have resulted in death or serious injury.

Here are just a few examples of emergency situations caused by marijuana:

1. March, 2015: Four high school students were hospitalized after eating brownies laced with marijuana hash oil. One student was actually found unresponsive in a school bathroom after eating a marijuana-laced brownie.

2. February, 2015: A 20-month-old Canadian toddler overdosed after eating a marijuana-laced cookie authorities say his father baked. The child survived, but suffered seizures and had to be admitted to a hospital.

3. February, 2015: News outlets report guests at Colorado hotels often leave unused food and beverages as tips for housekeeping staff. However, with the legalization of marijuana—and marijuana-infused foods—in Colorado, some guests are leaving marijuana edibles behind. One Breckenridge hotel employee reported accidentally overdosing when she ate a candy she did not realize was laced with marijuana.

4. February, 2015: An explosion occurred at an Arizona apartment complex. Witnesses indicated one of the people involved in the explosion was attempting to extract hash oil from marijuana using butane.

5. January, 2015: News outlets in Oregon reported a woman overdosed after she ate three gummy candies laced with marijuana.

6. December, 2014: A high school teacher in Maryland was hospitalized after a student gave her a brownie containing marijuana.

7. December, 2014: Two middle school students in Oklahoma were rushed to the hospital after one of them reportedly passed out following marijuana-use at school.

8. November, 2014: A Connecticut teen was taken to the hospital from school after she started having difficulty breathing

following ingestion of a marijuana-laced gummy bear.

9. June, 2014: According to *The Aspen Times*, a seven-year-old girl was taken to the hospital after eating marijuana-laced candy her mother brought home from work at an area hotel. The candy was left by a hotel guest—presumably as a tip.

10. March, 2014: A Colorado man attempting to extract hash oil from his marijuana was taken to the hospital after the butane used to extract the oil ignited.

11. December, 2013: A two-year-old in Colorado overdosed and was hospitalized after eating a cookie laced with marijuana. News outlet indicate the girl found the cookie in the yard of an apartment complex.

Recurring Themes: Kids and Accidental Overdoses

A recurring theme in many of these news stories is that children and teens are becoming severely ill after ingesting marijuana-laced food (often referred to as "edibles").

In July of 2013, researchers writing in *JAMA Pediatrics* determined accidental ingestion of marijuana by young children is on the rise and carries serious risks.

The greatest dangers appear to be toddlers and young children who accidentally find cookies or candy laced with marijuana and teens acquiring marijuana edibles at school without realizing how potent the drug-infused food is.

In both scenarios, children accidentally overdose on marijuana and must be taken to the ER. In some cases, as noted above, the children even pass out or become unresponsive.

A child who loses consciousness from marijuana overdose could easily fall and strike their head or suffer another serious injury. A teen who ingests a marijuana edible—without realizing its potency—before climbing behind the wheel of a car to drive away from school could easily be involved in a serious traffic accident.

Side-Effects May Including Exploding Apartments

A few of the cases we have cited include explosions caused by marijuana hash oil operations.

Many marijuana users produce their own hash oil at home by extracting the oil from marijuana using flammable chemicals like butane. In many cases, the room fills up with butane and is ignited by a stray spark, causing a serious explosion.

The people most at-risk are apartment dwellers. A person who lives in an apartment complex may have their home destroyed because a neighbor's hash oil operation exploded. In Washington, at least one person was actually killed as a result of a hash oil operation that exploded in a neighbor's apartment.

The legality of hash oil extraction is questionable under state laws in Washington, Colorado, and elsewhere. Colorado's Attorney General released an opined in December that home production of marijuana hash oil is illegal. However, many people disagree.

Regardless of its legality, it is clearly dangerous to the marijuana users and their family members and neighbors.

Conclusion: Marijuana Has Caused Far More Than 0 Deaths

Given the amount of evidence—both scientific and anecdotal—there simply does not seem to be any way around it: Marijuana is responsible for many deaths.

Moreover, marijuana has caused numerous medical emergencies that could have been fatal under different circumstances.

We continue to say it over and over again: Marijuana may be many things, but "harmless" simply is not one of them.

EVALUATING THE AUTHOR'S ARGUMENTS:

Compare this viewpoint to Chapter 1, Viewpoint 1, which discusses the safety of marijuana relative to alcohol. Where do they agree, and where do they do they differ? Which viewpoint seems more reliable to you? Why do you think this?

Viewpoint 3

Substance Abuse Is a Public Health Crisis

"All the huffing and puffing in the current war on drugs has not been able to blow down the nation's house of substance abuse and addiction."

Joseph A. Califano, Jr.

In the following viewpoint, the author addresses drug addiction. He includes a variety of illegal drugs as well as legal substances such as alcohol and tobacco. He connects drug and alcohol abuse to crime, child neglect, homelessness, and other problems. He argues that the health-care system should spend more money researching substance abuse and addiction and doctors should have better training on these issues. Health plans should cover substance abuse treatment. Courts and prisons should focus on addiction as a medical issue and offer treatment options. Joseph A. Califano, Jr. is a former US Secretary of Health, Education, and Welfare. He is also the founder and chairman of the National Center on Addiction and Substance Abuse at Columbia University.

"High Society: How Substance Abuse Ravages America and What to Do About It," by Joseph A. Califano, Jr., PublicAffairs. Reprinted by permission.

AS YOU READ, CONSIDER THE FOLLOWING QUESTIONS:
  1. How does dopamine affect the brain?
  2. According to this viewpoint, are those who abuse drugs likely to stay with one drug or to use a variety?
  3. How are smoking, drinking, and drug use related to mental health?

There was a time in our history—not so long ago—when smoking was cool, when seat belts were for sissies and when AIDS was seen as a death sentence for gay sex. Today our attitudes are profoundly different—with powerful and beneficial consequences. Smoking has been cut sharply, and so have the related deaths from lung cancer and heart disease. Auto safety measures have curbed the highway death and injury rate. AIDS is recognized as a serious illness rather than a social curse.

In all three cases, we fundamentally changed our attitudes and, as a result, took actions that greatly improved the quality of life for millions of people.

The time has come for a fundamental change in our attitude about the pervasive and pernicious role drug and alcohol abuse play in our society and a revolution in the way we deal with it.

Americans, comprising only 4 % of the world's population, consume 2/3 of the world's illegal drugs. The number of illegal drug users, which had dropped from a high of 25.4 million in 1979 to a quarter century low of 12 million in 1992, rose to 20.4 million in 2006. The number of teen illegal drug users, which had dropped from its 1979 high of 3.3 million to a low of 1.1 million in 1992, more than doubled to 2.5 million in 2006.

All the huffing and puffing in the current war on drugs has not been able to blow down the nation's house of substance abuse and addiction:

- 61 million Americans are hooked on cigarettes
- 16 to 20 million are addicted to alcohol or abuse it regularly
- More than 15 million abuse prescription drugs
- 15 million smoke marijuana

- 2.4 million use cocaine; 600,000 use crack
- Hundreds of thousands are hooked on heroin
- More than 750,000 are methamphetamine users
- 1 million use ecstasy and hallucinogens
- Almost 2 million of our children have used steroids
- 4.5 million teens abuse controlled prescription drugs like OxyContin, Ritalin, and Adderall to get high

The human misery that addiction and abuse cause can't be calculated. The consequences of this epidemic are severe.

Almost a quarter of a trillion dollars of the nation's yearly health-care bill is attributable to substance abuse and addiction.

Alcohol and other drug abuse is involved in most violent and property crimes, with 80% of the nation's adult inmates and juvenile arrestees either committing their offenses while high, stealing to buy drugs, violating alcohol or drug laws, having a history of substance abuse/addiction, or sharing some mix of these characteristics.

70% of abused and neglected children have alcohol or drug abusing parents.

90% of homeless are alcoholics or alcohol abusers; 60% abuse other drugs.

Half of the nation's college students binge drink and/or abuse illegal and prescription drugs. Nearly a quarter of them meet the medical criteria for alcohol and drug abuse and addiction. Cruel courtesy of excessive drinking, each year—700,000 students are injured, 100,000 are raped or sexually assaulted, and 1,700 are killed by alcohol poisoning or alcohol related injuries.

Addiction and the Brain

Statistically we have known for some time that teens who abuse alcohol and smoke marijuana are likelier to use drugs like cocaine and heroin. Now biomedical research and the brain imaging work of Dr. Nora Volkow, Director of the National Institute on Drug Abuse

Teen drug use more than doubled between 1992 and 2005, and the use of a variety of drugs due to social influences is common among kids and teenagers.

(NIDA), help explain why teens who play with the fire of cigarettes, alcohol and marijuana increase the chance they will get burned by the flames of heroin, cocaine and hallucinogens. All of these substances cause an increase in dopamine levels in the brain. As dopamine levels increase, an individual's feeling of pleasure increases. A growing body of science is finding that all these substances affect dopamine levels in the brain through similar pathways, and dopamine becomes less active in the brains of addicts who use drugs to trigger its release, a condition which in turn reinforces the need for the drug.

Studies by scientists in Italy reveal that marijuana affects levels of dopamine in the brain in a manner akin to heroin. Studies in the US have found that nicotine and alcohol (as well as cocaine) have a similar effect on dopamine levels through common pathways to the brain. This may explain why some scientists believe that nicotine makes the brain more accommodating to other drugs.

In essence, whatever the substance, the brains of addicts are "rewired," becoming predisposed to cravings. Dr. Joseph Frascella of NIDA points out that "in excessive behaviors such as compulsive drug abuse ... the brain is changed, reward circuits are disrupted, and the behavior eventually becomes involuntary ..."

These statistical and biological findings are underscored by the fact that most addicts are poly-drug abusers. Alcoholics are likely to abuse tranquilizers, sleeping pills, or other psychotropic drugs. Older teens who abuse prescription drugs are often found to be to be abusing other drugs as well. There are also social elements to the relationship among smoking, drinking and using illegal and prescription drugs, as well as to polydrug use, particularly among children and teens. Kids who seek the high from marijuana may also want to look for "better" highs from other drugs. As kids start using drugs, they may tend to hang out and share experiences with others who use different drugs. In a sense, these teens end up encouraging each other to use various drugs.

Of special importance is the need to recognize that for many teens, smoking, drinking, or drug use is often a symptom of incipient depression, anxiety or some other (usually undiagnosed) mental illness that hikes the youngster's risk of drug abuse.

Mental health problems go hand in hand with smoking, drinking and drug use for children and adults, and these problems can lead individuals to self-medicate with a variety of substances. Our current approach to substance abuse does not adequately recognize this.

Mounting a Revolution

We must recognize that substance abuse and addiction is a disease, not a moral failing or easily abandoned self-indulgence. We must recognize that it is a complex disease with neurological, physical, emotional and spiritual components. We must recognize its impact on the most intractable domestic problems we confront. With such acceptance and recognition, we will appreciate the benefits of a revolution.

In the Health-care System—The National Institutes of Health spend $13 billion a year on research for cancer, strokes, cardio-vascular and respiratory diseases and AIDS, but only 1/10 of that amount to study substance abuse and addiction—the largest single cause and excacerbator of this quintet of killers and cripplers. It is time for a revolution in health-care: the creation of the National Institute on Addiction, with a budget of at least $3 billion a year to conduct a "Manhattan Project"-style research initiative identifying the causes and cures of substance abuse and addiction.

Courses in substance abuse and addiction should be a compulsory part of medical school curriculums. Physicians should be trained to diagnose the disease and refer patients for treatment. States and medical societies should establish professional standards for treatment counselors and accreditation systems to certify treatment facilities. Public and private health plans should cover substance abuse treatment and pay doctors to talk to patients.

Only through professionalizing the treatment system will we be able to bring it fully into the medical care system, which, in turn, is key to obtaining parity of coverage.

In the Justice System—Our nation's prison system is as anachronistic as the debtor prisons in Charles Dickens' day. Prosecutors, courts and prisons must seize the opportunity to reclaim hundreds of thousands of addicts by using the criminal justice system to offer effective treatment for all who need it and incentives for them to achieve and maintain sobriety. Successfully treating and training inmates could deliver the greatest reduction in criminal activity in the nation's history. Experts estimate that the number of crimes committed by a drug addict range from 89 to 191 annually.

In the Social Service System—Parental substance abuse accounts for $23 billion in the nation's child welfare spending, and most domestic violence involves alcohol or other drugs. The time has come for a complete overhaul of family court, adoption and foster care systems in order to better deal with alcohol and drug abusing parents and partners. The only way we will rehabilitate our nation's homeless population is by investing in substance abuse and mental health treatment.

In the Education System—Schools, from elementary through college, should include age appropriate education about all substance abuse involving tobacco, alcohol, prescription and illegal drugs as they do about other health matters from hygiene to STDs.

Prevention should be "laser beamed" on children. 16 years of research at CASAColumbia finds that a child who gets through age 21 without smoking, using illegal drugs, or abusing alcohol is virtually certain never to do so.

It is time to end the denial and stamp out the stigma associated with substance abuse and addiction, and to finally commit the energy and resources to confront a plague that has maimed and killed more Americans than all our wars, natural catastrophes and traffic accidents combined.

In his monumental study of history, the brilliant British historian Arnold Toynbee found that the great civilizations were destroyed not by an external enemy, but from within. "Civilizations," he said, "die from suicide, not by murder." Of all the internal dangers our nation faces, none possess a greater threat to our children and families and none is complicit in more domestic ills than substance abuse and addiction.

This is our enemy within.

The judgment of history will be harsh if we fail to defeat that enemy—and deservedly so, when the stakes are our children and there is so much we can do to help them.

EVALUATING THE AUTHOR'S ARGUMENTS:

This viewpoint argues that we should adjust the way we think about drug use and abuse, including the abuse of alcohol and marijuana. How does the current trend toward legalizing marijuana fit in with this philosophy? Do you think a social change would have the effects this author suggests? Why or why not?

Legalization Won't Get Rid of Illegal Pot

Chris Frey

"The stuff the government is going to sell; it'll be weaker, like the difference between light beer and regular beer, or even liquor."

In the following viewpoint, a reporter interviews two marijuana dealers in Canada. The reporter asked how legalization would affect the dealers' businesses. The dealers note that prices are dropping as more people get into the business. However, legal marijuana is regulated and taxed by the government. If it is priced too high, people may continue buying from the illegal black market. The interview subjects debate whether some dealers will move into harder drugs, which may lead to more violence. This viewpoint was written for the *Guardian*, a British daily newspaper. Chris Frey is a Canadian journalist who serves as the Toronto correspondent for *Monocle Magazine*. He has written for the *Guardian* and *Globe and Mail*, among other publications.

"'I Deliver To Your House': Pot Dealers On Why Legalization Won't Kill the Black Market," by Chris Frey, Guardian News & Media Limited, June 7, 2018. Reprinted by permission.

AS YOU READ, CONSIDER THE FOLLOWING QUESTIONS:
1. Why did legalization make it harder for some Canadian pot dealers to make money?
2. Why might some people buy from the black market even if pot is legally available?
3. Will marijuana use greatly increase once it's legal, according to this viewpoint?

It's a case of My Guy versus The Man: who will you buy your pot from? As legalization looms, governments across Canada are angling for a generous slice of what was a $5.7bn marijuana business in 2017. The rules vary across the country—some provinces will permit licensed private retailers; others will sell pot exclusively through government stores—but success will ultimately depend on just one thing: beating the black market.

So is that black market worried? Two Toronto-based dealers agreed to speak with us. Gord, 44, has been selling marijuana full-time since he was 16, and his business had the trappings of a retail empire, with business cards advertising Smiley Face Delivery. Ray, 45, who began selling 17 years ago, is more modest in his ambitions. "I have a day job," he said. "I do this for the extras, so I can take my wife out to an expensive dinner. I don't really look at it as a serious business. It's as much a cultural thing."

How will legalization affect your business?

Gord: Ever since the government started talking about legalization and all these [illegal storefront] dispensaries opened up, the profit margins have decreased. All the years I've been selling, the price never changed very much—like around C$250 to $300 per ounce for the really good stuff. Now I'm supposed to lower my prices down to $200 or less. And you have this younger generation coming up that's used to the idea of stores and getting pot anywhere. In the old days you had a drug dealer and you held on to him. He's like your doctor or mechanic: once you got a good one you held on to him. The loyalty thing is dead now. So a lot of the bigger dealers are saying:

Even if marijuana is legalized, some factors could cause the illegal marijuana market to continue to exist.

"You know what? My time's done, it's time to retire." The last year I've taken a pretty big hit on the finances so I've been looking at an exit strategy. Which is kind of just exiting slowly, trimming the fat, only helping out the people who've been the most loyal.

Ray: Five years ago, it was different. Some people were definitely making more money, simply because there were fewer people in the industry, but now their income has dropped. I operate at a smaller scale, I do this because I enjoy it and I make some extra money. So for me it's great that the government is coming in—I'm happy as sh*t. The reason why is now they're going to shut down the dispensaries and they're my biggest competition. Plus, the THC content of the pot the government will be selling is going to be 20% or less. The guys I know selling commercially can't wait till the government comes in.

What's the key factor in determining whether the black market will continue? Is it price? Quality? Ease of access? Ministers have discussed $10/g, but the average street price nationally is only $7/g.

Ray: Price is 90% of it. The majority of people aren't connoisseurs and don't have a lot of money to spend on pot. They want a good deal and don't care, or know, much about quality. If the government prices pot too high you're not giving those people an option, so they will stick with the black market. I'm still going to deal with the regular people I deal with: people who go to work everyday and just want to smoke a little pot, but don't want to pay the astronomical prices the government is going to charge.

Gord: You got to include all the tax [on government pot] as well. It'll be like smokes and alcohol: whenever they need more money, "sin taxes" will be the first thing they'll increase.

What about convenience? Alberta is talking about having 250 storefronts, but Quebec only 15—to service 8.2 million people.

Ray: We've had this period in Toronto where it seemed like illegal dispensaries were opening on almost every block. Now Ontario will have, what, something like 40 [government-operated] stores to start? There's no way they'll be as convenient for consumers. Once they shut down the illegal dispensaries it will just level the playing field for dealers like me. And I deliver to your home.

What do [you] expect from the quality of government weed?

Gord: It's going to be mass produced, like Labatt's beer or Budweiser, all off-the-shelf, generic, it'll taste the same every time. It won't have much strength so it's like you're really just buying a flavour. Maybe you can produce an excellent kush that's 29% THC, but no, they government will tell you, you have to do it this way.

Ray: The stuff the government is going to sell; it'll be weaker, like the difference between light beer and regular beer, or even liquor.

After all these years of very lax enforcement, does it feel as if pot dealers are about to be recriminalized? Do dealers now have new reason to fear the police?

Ray: I've never really had to worry and I'm not worried now. I have friends in law enforcement, and generally they look [at marijuana prohibition] like it's ridiculous, the dumbest thing ever. They can tell if someone is organized crime or it's just some local guy growing a basement full of pot and selling to his friends. If it's organized crime, then OK, that changes everything, but for the local guy? They'd rather leave that guy alone. They have other street drugs to worry about: fentanyl, cocaine … and guns.

Gord: In my experience, the fear only comes when you start to sell the hard, poisonous drugs. I can only think of one time since I started selling at 16 when I was ever really scared, and that was [when] I was driving through [a police drunk-driving checkpoint] with 15lbs of weed in my car. That scared me. But that was the only time.

If the bigger dealers get squeezed out by the market, where will they go?

Gord: I can't be the only person in this country who's noticed a direct correlation between the talk of legalization and the increase in fentanyl and heroin and gun violence. You're already seeing more killings, more problems [associated with harder drugs]. Some of us have our morals and ethics we follow: we won't go into the stuff that will kill people. Other dealers I know have branched out into other markets.

Ray: For sure you will have some small percentage of dealers—especially those strictly in it for the money—move into harder drugs, but that's like any industry when you're getting squeezed out. You become willing to take bigger risks. Everyone in the marijuana business is pretty decent for the most part. Maybe you'll get the odd guy who wants to be a badass, who thinks marijuana's too soft and they're not making enough money. A percentage of those guys will move into selling crack, cocaine, pills, whatever.

Is there as much money to be made in legal pot as everyone now seems to think?

Ray: I don't really see it. Whether the dispensaries are there, or whether the government comes in, there's still about the same number of people smoking. Maybe as kids turn 19 and they're allowed to buy at a government store, you might get a 10% spike in the people who will try it—but not everybody's going to try it and like it. You're not going to get this astronomical increase.

Will a diminished black market affect the broader economy?

Gord: Unfortunately, you take away a black market and you hurt the economy, in ways you'll never understand, because it's so much easier to spend money that's not taxed than explain where your money has come from. Our black market money is what stimulated all the fun things in life. The cars and boats nobody could afford to buy otherwise. The dealer never worried about going out for a $400 lunch with his two halfwit buddies because he knew there'd be another $400 later that day.

With the elimination of dispensaries, do you see an opportunity to grow your business?

Ray: I would love to grow my business, but I'm too lazy. Is it really worth the extra dollar to run around and kill yourself that much more? I have one friend who is ambitious about it, he's working all day and night, driving around. He loves to buy his materialistic things, going on vacation. For dealers like me and most of my friends—if we make a buck today then great. It's just supplementing our income. I have a day job, I do this for the extras, so I can take my wife out to an expensive dinner. I don't look at it as business: it's a cultural thing. If I can make a dollar off it I will—if not, I'm still going to smoke. I mean, a person who smokes pot is pretty chill to begin with.

EVALUATING THE AUTHOR'S ARGUMENTS:

Some people claim that if people can access legal marijuana, illegal drug dealers will go out of business, and crime will drop. How do you feel about that theory after reading this viewpoint? Does it seem likely that legalizing marijuana will reduce crime, increase crime, or make no difference?

Chapter 3

How Should Marijuana Be Legalized?

Today, many Americans support the legalization of marijuana.

Following the Law May Not Save You

> "Until federal law changes, patients across the country face dire choices between violating the laws of their country and treating their illness."

Americans for Safe Access

The following excerpted viewpoint discusses legal problems with medical cannabis. Marijuana is illegal nationwide, according to the federal government, yet many states have passed laws making marijuana or the component CBD legal for at least some uses. This viewpoint notes that patients and providers can be arrested, which can lead to further discrimination. The authors attempt to educate patients and suppliers of medical cannabis about the laws. They recommend that people follow the laws as closely as possible, whenever possible. Still, they warn people that they may suffer serious consequences even if they follow the laws. Americans for Safe Access (ASA) is an organization that aims to ensure safe and legal access to cannabis for therapeutic uses and research.

AS YOU READ, CONSIDER THE FOLLOWING QUESTIONS:

1. Why can the federal government prosecute people for activities that are legal in their state?
2. What are some of the forms of discrimination someone may face if they're convicted of a drug crime?
3. Does it help if someone can claim they were using marijuana for medical reasons?

Medical cannabis patients and their providers are vulnerable to federal and state raids, arrest, prosecution, and incarceration. As a result, these individuals may suffer pervasive discrimination in employment, child custody, housing, public accommodation, education and medical care. Laws protecting patients and their providers vary from state to state and, in some cases, may vary from county to county. Many individuals choose to break outdated state laws that do not account for medical use or their access. And no matter what state you are living in, medical cannabis patients and their providers are always violating federal law.

Making the choice to participate in a medical cannabis program or to resist current laws should be done with thoughtful consideration. Following the law in your local area may not always protect you from law enforcement encounters, and the more you know about your rights, the more likely you will be to have a successful encounter with law enforcement. It's important to also remember that the best law enforcement encounter is the one that never happens.

The information found in this section is meant to educate patients and their providers about the existing federal laws, how to avoid law enforcement encounters, how to be prepared for encounters, how to understand your rights during encounters, and how to navigate the legal system after an encounter. After you understand this material, be sure to share this information with your family, friends, or anyone who may be at risk.

Know the Laws

State Laws

Medical cannabis laws vary from state to state. The section on state laws summarizes some of the key information, with links to more details. If you live in a medical cannabis state, consult AmericansForSafeAccess. org/LocalResources to find out about your state's medical cannabis program. Finally, consult local laws and regulations to make sure that you are adhering to any guidelines developed by your county or city. Following each law to the letter may not prevent you from having a law enforcement encounter, but it will help you have a successful one.

Federal Laws

Despite the promises made by the Obama campaign and the memo issued in 2009 by the Department of Justice, medical cannabis remains illegal at the federal level and carries severe penalties. Federal interference with state medical cannabis programs can happen in every state, and there is no "medical" defense within the federal justice system. If you're participating in your state's medical cannabis program, you are in direct violation of federal law. It is important to remember that even though the media has hyped the meager promises made by different parts of the federal government, patients have no federal protection and are still at risk. Until federal law changes, patients across the country face dire choices between violating the laws of their country and treating their illness with the medication deemed most appropriate by their physician.

The federal government regulates drugs through the Controlled Substances Act (CSA) (21 U.S.C. § 811), which places every controlled substance in a schedule, according to its relative potential for abuse and medicinal value. Under the CSA, cannabis is classified as a Schedule I drug, which means that the federal government views cannabis as being highly addictive and having no medical value. Doctors may not "prescribe" cannabis for medical use, though they can "recommend" or "approve" its use under the First Amendment. This recommendation or approval does not provide patients with any sort of legal protection under federal law, but it may be the basis for legal protection under state law. Under federal law, you and your doctor are free to discuss the possible benefits and side effects of medical cannabis.

The Drug Enforcement Administration (DEA), charged with enforcing federal drug laws, has taken a substantial interest in individual medical cannabis patients and caregivers, particularly those involved in large cultivation and distribution operations. Over the past decade, hundreds of people have been the targets of federal enforcement actions. Many of them have been arrested and had property seized. More than a hundred medical cannabis providers are currently in prison or are facing charges.

Federal cannabis laws are very serious, and punishment for people found guilty is frequently severe. Federal judges have ruled that medical necessity cannot be used as a defense. In fact, medical cannabis

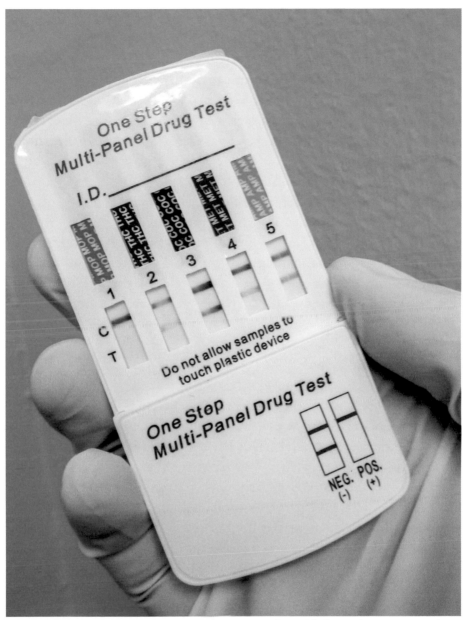

Even if marijuana is legalized at the state level, it is still possible for employers to test and punish those who use marijuana under federal law.

cannot even be mentioned during a federal trial. Patients may not use evidence related to their state's medical cannabis program, their doctor's recommendation, their illness, or anything else related to medical cannabis.

Federal sentencing guidelines take into account not only the amount of cannabis but also past convictions. Not all cannabis convictions require jail time under federal sentencing guidelines, but some do and all are eligible for imprisonment. If convicted and sentenced to jail, a minimum of 85% of that sentence must be served. The greater the quantity of cannabis involved, the more likely one is to be sentenced to jail time, as opposed to probation or alternative sentencing.

In addition to the sentencing guidelines, there are statutory mandatory minimum sentences, which primarily target offenses involving large quantities of cannabis. There is a five-year mandatory minimum for cultivation of 100 plants or possession of 100kgs, and there is a ten-year mandatory minimum for these offenses if the defendant has a prior felony drug conviction. Cultivation of 1,000 plants or possession of 1,000kg triggers a ten-year mandatory minimum, with a twenty-year mandatory sentence if the defendant has one prior felony drug conviction, and a life sentence with two prior felony drug convictions.

The 2005 US Supreme Court decision in US v. Booker altered the mandatory minimums to make them effectively advisory, requiring a sentencing court to consider Guidelines ranges. Nonetheless, to avoid a five-year federal sentence, it is advisable to cultivate well below 100 plants, including any rooted cuttings or clones.

Low-level federal offenders, even with multiple prior convictions, may end up with probation for the entire sentence of one to twelve months and no jail time required. Possession of over one kg (2.2 lbs.) of cannabis with no prior convictions carries a sentence of six to twelve months with a possibility of probation and alternative sentencing. Over 2.5 kg with no criminal record carries a sentence of at least six months in jail; with multiple prior convictions, a sentence might be up to two years to three years in prison with no chance for probation.

Keep in mind that even though medical cannabis protections may exist in your state, the federal government allows no medical defense to possession, cultivation, or distribution charges. Even though the Obama administration and the Department of Justice have made statements that prosecuting patients is a low priority, patients and providers are still being harassed, raided, arrested, and convicted throughout the US Until federal law changes, participating in your state's medical cannabis program still carries some risk.

Other Applicable Laws
School Zones
Patients and providers should avoid possession and cultivation of cannabis in school zones—a 1,000-foot radius around any school, including any daycare facility—as there are typically additional penalties for the possession, use, and cultivation of cannabis near schools, whether it is for medical or recreational use. Some state medical cannabis laws have limitations on "sensitive use" areas, limiting cultivation, use, and possession of medical cannabis within a specific amount of space of a school, playground, etc. Most use the federal 1,000-foot radius but some mandate up to 1,500 feet. In addition, keep in mind that Drug Free School Zone laws can double the maximum sentences in federal court, where the mention of "medical cannabis" is prohibited.

Firearms
Firearms can result in harsher federal sentencing and may draw attention to patients. Even if your state protects patients' right to safe access to medical cannabis, the presence of firearms may increase the chances of an adverse state or federal law enforcement encounter, and harsher sentences if convicted. Again, the best law enforcement encounter is the one that never happens.

Under federal law, "any person who, during any drug trafficking crime for which the person may be prosecuted in a court of the United States, uses or carries a firearm, or who, in furtherance of any such crime, possesses a firearm, shall:

1. Be sentenced to a term of imprisonment of not less than 5 years;
2. If the firearm is brandished, not less than 7 years; and
3. If the firearm is discharged, not less than 10 years."

Although the US Constitution confers a right to carry firearms, we have seen many patients face extreme legal consequences for having firearms in addition to plants.

In addition, the memo issued by the Department of Justice in 2009, which was intended to provide the US Attorneys' Offices with guidance on the prosecution of medical cannabis patients and providers, specifically mentions the presence of firearms as an example of "potential federal interest" that probably falls outside of "clear and unambiguous compliance" with underlying state law. In other words, beyond the sentencing enhancements, the presence of firearms makes patients and providers a more likely target for federal prosecution.

ASA strongly advises that, if you are a medical cannabis patient, do not carry firearms or keep them on your property or allow others to do so.

Civil Asset Forfeiture

Federal law provides for the forfeiture of property and profits obtained through or used in the commission of felony drug offenses. Prosecutors have incentives to include forfeiture offences in all drug indictments. Forfeiture can apply to landlords who rent to people considered in violation of federal law, and therefore can also be used to intimidate the landlords of patients who cultivate or use their medicine on the premises. It should be noted, however, that landlords do have defenses available to them in these types of civil actions, and that they are rarely targets of forfeiture if they themselves were not participating in the use, possession, or cultivation of medical cannabis.

Best Law Enforcement Encounter Is the Encounter that Never Occurs

While your state may have extensive laws that protect your right to use medical cannabis, many law enforcement officers still believe that medical cannabis is a "sham" and that all use of cannabis is recreational use. Law enforcement officers often seize medicine, harass patients, issue citations, and even arrest patients for exercising their rights. Carry your doctor's written recommendation and/or state-issued ID Card (following your state's requirement) at all times, but do not present it to law enforcement unless accused of a cannabis-related crime. Dealing with criminal charges and/or getting your medicine back can be stressful and costly, and may cause you to be "outed" as a medical cannabis patient. That's why we say that the best law enforcement encounter is the one that never occurs. If you follow these tips, you will be that much less likely to be harassed by law enforcement.

[...]

EVALUATING THE AUTHOR'S ARGUMENTS:

This viewpoint describes some of the challenges that arise when state laws differ from federal laws. Do you agree that the situation is problematic? What do you think should happen with marijuana laws based on what you've read in this viewpoint?

"If the end were truly better medications for patients perhaps it would be simpler and safer to just develop an efficient, effective delivery system for the clinically valuable components of this ubiquitous plant."

Medical Marijuana Should Be Treated Like Any Other Drug

William H. Foster

The following viewpoint notes that marijuana is becoming legal through votes in various states, and some medical forms of THC have been available medically for years. Yet people may still prefer to smoke pot, as the effects are more powerful and happen faster. However, marijuana has not gone through the typical testing and approval processes required of a drug. The author suggests that people pushing for medical marijuana laws really want complete legalization. He suggests that prescribing marijuana as a medicine is a way to hide the end goal. The National Center on Addiction and Substance Abuse is now called Center on Addiction. This organization offers help in the prevention and treatment of drug addiction. William H. Foster is the president and CEO of the Center on Addiction.

"Marijuana Legalization: How Should Medical Marijuana Be Regulated?" by William H. Foster, The National Center on Addiction and Substance Abuse, December 11, 2010. Reprinted by permission.

AS YOU READ, CONSIDER THE FOLLOWING QUESTIONS:
1. How does the Federal Drug Administration (FDA) usually approve a drug?
2. Why is inhaling marijuana smoke different from taking a pill?
3. Has marijuana been tested and approved as effective and safe by the FDA?

Well, the debate continues apace. Fourteen states and the District of Columbia have already voted to legalize medical marijuana. And 8 states continue to consider the matter. If these considerations end up in the affirmative, we will have reached a point where the citizens in almost half of our states will have decided the medical merits and clinical value of a federally designated and controlled substance through the ballot box. No FDA review and approval required for this particular prescription medicine.

Through our nation's democratic political processes voters will have functionally certified the clinical effectiveness and "do no harm" character of a psychopharmacological treatment for both acute and chronic maladies, rather than through the use of our existing scientific review processes and well understood procedures of our FDA.

No carefully designed and implemented controlled clinical trials, no need for health-risk assessments, no encompassing epidemiological evidence required. We will have replaced them, in the case of medical marijuana, with some good doses of political rhetoric, numerous provocative "talking head" media debates, many formal legislative and public hearings and a final certification of medicinal safety and efficacy by majority vote.

I find this fascinating! It is certainly a legitimate question to ask as to whether marijuana has clinically therapeutic and/or curative characteristics. There is nothing wrong with a serious consideration as to whether this easily grown plant has merits as prescription medication for a select number of illnesses and health conditions, acute or chronic.

For many years now one of the plant's key ingredients, delta-9-tetrahydrocannabinol or THC, has been available to prescribers and

In states that have legalized medical marijuana, it can be obtained at a marijuana dispensary. However, despite its legal status, marijuana has not been approved by the FDA.

patients in the form of the cannabinoid pills Marinol and Cesamet. A major complaint of patients, however, has been the inefficiency and ineffectiveness of the means of delivery of these medications. They are swallowed and as a result are slow to act and depress both the psychoactive and medicinal effects of the pill's THC. In contrast when marijuana is smoked, as provided by voter authorized medical marijuana dispensaries, the active components of the plant are efficiently inhaled directly into the lungs and immediately into the blood stream—purportedly providing both the psychoactive as well as the medicinal effects of the marijuana.

So, let's pretend for a moment that an efficient, clinically effective respiratory means of delivering only the medically beneficial components of marijuana were to be developed in some pharmaceutical laboratory. Wouldn't it be reasonable for us to expect that because of its therapeutic import, such a new medication, with its unique respiratory delivery system, would require FDA review and approval, subsequent prescriptive distribution and then clinical management through on-going medical supervision, as is currently the case with Marinol and Cesamet?

Then we could retreat from our peculiar practice of authorizing prescription medicines through the ballot box. And we could avoid the unintended consequences of our emerging medical marijuana distribution system—a system vulnerable to concerns such as uncontrolled dose amounts; poorly monitored treatment protocols, on-going exposure to high

levels of carcinogens, higher than any commercially sold cigarette; heightened probability of accidents due to intoxication; and almost certain diversion and subsequent increased availability for recreational rather than medicinal use. Prescribed, distributed, smoked medical marijuana may have its clinical value. But it does have its downsides—some potentially serious ones.

Let's step back for a moment and look at what else could be going on here. Let's stipulate that as a carefully crafted tactical first step toward someone's ultimate objective of legalization that the medical marijuana political gambit is not a bad first act. For how many in the political arena can ultimately stand against the winds blowing in favor of helping the seriously sick and those with chronic pain?

If the end were truly better medications for patients perhaps it would be simpler and safer to just develop an efficient, effective delivery system for the clinically valuable components of this ubiquitous plant. Just like we have with medicinal derivatives from other plants such as those crafted from the poppy.

But, if legalization is in fact the ultimate intent of this current scripting of the American political psyche and landscape regarding medical marijuana, then let's be clear. Let us distinguish ends from means. Let's not be too naive regarding what this may actually be about.

If the end of this political gambit is legalization perhaps we should deal with the complex public health and medical matters associated with that proposition directly and thoughtfully. Not through the smoke screen of politically approved medical marijuana distraction, a distraction that is most likely just a means to another more problematic end.

EVALUATING THE AUTHOR'S ARGUMENTS:

In this viewpoint, the author suggests that medical marijuana should go through the typical approval processes required for a drug. How does he support his views? Does it make a difference if marijuana may be legalized for recreational use anyway? Why or why not?

Laws Should Be Changed to Allow Medical Research

Sam Méndez

"Research will be heavily restricted for as long as cannabis remains on Schedule I."

In the following viewpoint, the author notes that a 2016 DEA decision allows more groups to produce marijuana cannabis for research. This decision will likely lead to a better scientific understanding of how cannabis affects the body and how it can be used as a medicine. However, the process to get a license to research a Schedule I drug is difficult. That restriction will continue to limit research. The author also describes some alternatives to how cannabis could be reclassified. These changes might allow for more research to show when and how cannabis has medical value. Sam Méndez is director of the Cannabis Law and Policy Project at the University of Washington.

This year's election season was historic in more ways than one. An unprecedented nine states considered liberalizing cannabis laws, and here's how it broke down: California, Massachusetts, Maine and Nevada saw their ballot measures pass, bringing the total number of states with legal adult-use cannabis laws up to eight. Arizona's ballot measure failed to pass.

Further, Florida, Arkansas, North Dakota, Montana passed their medical cannabis ballot measures, bringing the total number of states with medical cannabis laws up to 28 (Montana's measure expanded its already existing laws).

To many in the cannabis reform movement, this is cause for celebration. California is easily the biggest news here, being the sixth largest economy in the world and dwarfing all current cannabis-legal states combined. That's a big domino to fall.

The DEA Isn't Rescheduling Cannabis, for Now

The trend toward legalization is sweeping the country, and it doesn't seem to be slowing. This might lead some who support the movement to assume legal pot nationwide is a foregone conclusion, but that's far from the truth.

The legality, or illegality, of cannabis at the federal level hasn't changed at all, where it is still classified as a Schedule I drug under the Controlled Substances Act. That means that lawmakers consider cannabis a substance with a high potential for abuse and no accepted medical use. Schedule I also includes drugs like heroin, LSD and ecstasy.

Despite many rumors that the Drug Enforcement Administration would reschedule cannabis to Schedule II earlier this year, meaning that it would legally have accepted medical uses, the DEA reaffirmed its decades-old position in August. Though many activists argue fervently for cannabis' medical uses, the science of it gets rather complicated. The federal government likely will change cannabis' legal status at some point, but nobody knows when that'll happen.

The DEA's decision had an important caveat though. It allowed new entities to apply to become producers and distributors of cannabis for research purposes.

Up until now, under federal law, the University of Mississippi was the sole entity allowed to produce cannabis for research purposes. This was a significant barrier for researchers because the University of Mississippi cultivated a limited number of cannabis strains that aren't reflective on the vast diversity of strains that are consumed by users.

With more entities (likely other universities) doing this work, there will be a greater diversity of cannabis plants that can be researched. Unfortunately, the process to get a license to research a Schedule I drug is far more difficult than one of a lower scheduled drug, so research will be heavily restricted for as long as cannabis remains on Schedule I.

Promoting Research Could Have a Bigger Effect

John Hudak of the Brookings Institution argued that the DEA's decision to allow more entities to produce marijuana cannabis for research was actually more important than rescheduling. Rescheduling would not have as much of an effect as many believe, while promoting research will lead to a better scientific understanding of cannabis' medicinal value—and risk. This, Hudak argues, will then likely lead to rescheduling anyway.

Hudak is right in the sense that the federal government will eventually have to reform its stance as more and more states go legal. But how exactly will that occur?

As Hudak also pointed out, simply putting cannabis on Schedule II does far less than many believe. That would place cannabis on a list with drugs like oxycodone and morphine, which can be prescribed but aren't sold recreationally in stores. That would allow physicians to prescribe cannabis and could lead to interesting and complicated ramifications.

The Food and Drug Administration would then begin regulating it, and you can expect the pharmaceutical industry to capitalize on cannabis

Though marijuana use was once stigmatized, it is now legal to use in many states. It is no longer taboo to discuss or advertise.

as well. If people are worried about "Big Marijuana," just wait until Big Pharma gets involved. But it would do little to legitimize the recreational systems that already exist in states like Washington and Colorado.

A Schedule II placement would also do nothing to change the industry's tax headache. An Internal Revenue Code provision that prevents cannabis businesses from making normal business deductions, and which takes a huge bite into their profits.

Cannabis would have to be on Schedule III—which includes drugs like anabolic steroids and Tylenol containing codeine—or below for that provision to no longer apply. Legalization advocates like the National Organization for the Reform of Marijuana Laws argue that cannabis should be descheduled—not rescheduled—so that it would be regulated more like alcohol.

So how will federal reform take place? It can either come from the DEA or from Congress. But the DEA has shown little sign that it would reschedule cannabis, and given partisan gridlock in Washington, we can't expect Congress to take action on something as momentous as significant drug reform any time soon.

Reforming Without Rescheduling

One interesting alternative has been proposed by famed legal theorist Erwin Chemerinsky and his colleagues. The federal government would take a "cooperative federalism" approach. That would allow states to further develop new drug laws without conflicting with federal laws, as they do now.

This would work by creating an opt-out system, where states can be left to craft their own cannabis policy so long as they meet certain federal requirements. This would allow the states to opt out of the Controlled Substances Act with respect to cannabis. The act would still apply as usual in states that don't have their own cannabis policy.

This would legally allow both federal and state policies to coexist without having to reschedule cannabis. Chemerinsky points out that the Clean Air Act already acts in this way, where the federal government regulates air pollution but also allows states to adopt their own regulations if they meet certain federal requirements.

History was certainly made this election season, but the story is far from over. There's little indication that the trend of legalization will be reversed as more US states legalize. How the US government will act will perhaps be the climax of this policy story. It is difficult to know how—and when—that will occur.

EVALUATING THE AUTHOR'S ARGUMENTS:

In his viewpoint, the author discusses several possible changes to how cannabis should be classified. Which option does he seem to think is best, if any? Which do you think is best? Why do you think this?

Viewpoint 4

Marijuana Must Be Regulated for Public Safety

American Public Health Association

"The preponderance of evidence supports regulating marijuana as an important public health policy."

The following excerpted viewpoint considers some health challenges legalized marijuana may introduce. Currently, marijuana is not carefully controlled for quality or strength. It may contain additional harmful substances. The health effects of using marijuana are not fully understood, but may be serious. Children and teenagers in particular may suffer harm from using marijuana. This viewpoint also suggests some ways to address these issues. Many of the suggestions are similar to the restrictions placed on alcohol and tobacco. History shows that these restrictions can be effective in reducing the use and misuse of harmful substances. The American Public Health Association (APHA) is a professional organization for public health professionals.

"Regulating Commercially Legalized Marijuana as a Public Health Priority," American Public Health Association, November 18, 2014. Reprinted by permission.

AS YOU READ, CONSIDER THE FOLLOWING QUESTIONS:
1. What is the advantage of standardizing the potency and quality of a substance?
2. Do warning labels affect consumers' behavior?
3. How can restricting advertising affect the use of controlled substances?

[...]

With the onset of commercial legalization of marijuana, several questions arise: How will access and availability to adolescents be prevented? How will the impact on vulnerable populations be addressed? What types of quality and informational controls will protect consumers? How will unwanted exposures and driving impairment be handled?

Increased Availability

The national Monitoring the Future study has consistently shown that roughly 80% of 12th graders, 70% of 10th graders, and 40% of 8th graders in the United States report that marijuana is either "fairly easy" or "very easy" to obtain. Concern exists that commercial legalization will increase the availability of marijuana to adolescents. The density of marijuana retailers is also an issue that needs to be addressed by regulation. If retailers congregate in a few locations, the populations in those areas will be more exposed to use, misuse, and abuse of marijuana. Advertising by retailers will also need to be examined, especially in light of studies revealing that alcohol and tobacco advertising is more prevalent in communities of color and areas of lower income.

Passive Exposures

As with the smoking of tobacco, passive exposure to marijuana smoke among children, tenants of multiunit housing developments, and nonsmokers is a concern. Protection for workers who cultivate commercial marijuana is also a concern since they may be exposed to pesticides, fertilizers, and other unhealthy adulterants. For example, a group of workers at a medical marijuana cultivator in Maine filed a complaint with the National Labor Relations Board because of the cultivator's use of pesticides and the workers' exposure to mold.

Quality Control and Consumer Protection

Because marijuana remains illicit, there are no mechanisms for its production to be monitored, its potency and quality to be standardized and tested, or its labeling for potential health effects before being sold. Research has shown that potency can vary widely depending on the strain of marijuana and that the drug can be contaminated by fungi and bacteria, heavy metals, pesticides, growth enhancers, and substances (e.g., glass beads) that are intended to increase its weight or give the appearance of a higher potency. A failure to provide accurate and credible information about marijuana's potency and quality can lead to consumer harm.

[...]

Motor Vehicle Safety

One "meta-analysis of studies examining acute cannabis consumption and motor vehicle collisions [revealed] a near doubling of risk of a driver being involved in a motor vehicle collision resulting in serious injury or death."

[...]

Health Effects

The health effects of smoking marijuana are not fully understood. A recent study published in the *Journal of the American Medical Association* investigated the association between marijuana use and lung function in a cohort of more than 5,000 US adults over a period of 20 years; the study's results suggested that "occasional use of marijuana ... may not be associated with adverse consequences on pulmonary function." However, marijuana, like tobacco, contains toxic gases and other substances that can cause harm to the pulmonary system. A recent review published in the *New England Journal of Medicine* documented the effects of long-term or heavy marijuana use, including addiction for

The United States of marijuana

Almost 60 percent of the US population lives in states where the sale and use of marijuana is legal to some extent

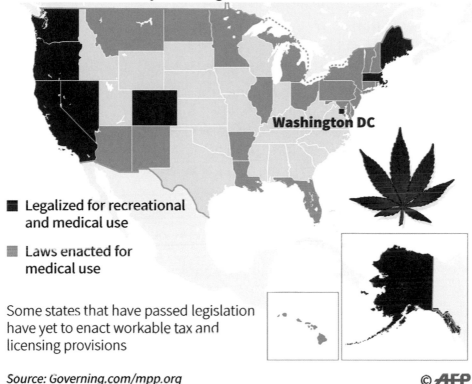

Washington DC

■ **Legalized for recreational and medical use**

▥ **Laws enacted for medical use**

Some states that have passed legislation have yet to enact workable tax and licensing provisions

Source: Governing.com/mpp.org

© *AFP*

Despite the fact that it is still illegal at the federal level, the number of states that have legalized marijuana continues to grow each year.

about 9% of all regular users, altered brain development and cognitive impairment among adolescent users, chronic bronchitis symptoms, and an increased risk of chronic psychosis disorders among those who are predisposed to such orders. Short-term effects include short-term memory impairment, impaired motor control, altered judgment, and, for some, paranoia and psychosis with high doses.

Strategies to Address the Problem

Jurisdictions that legalize or consider the legalization of commercial marijuana should develop, adopt, monitor, and evaluate regulatory schemes for marijuana production, sale, and use that protect and promote public health.

[...]

Age Restrictions

Age restrictions and enhanced enforcement of age restrictions can be used to limit the use of marijuana by adolescents, just as they are used to control tobacco use and alcohol use among adolescents, which have declined significantly over the past several years. According to the Monitoring the Future study, daily use of cigarettes by 12th graders decreased from 26.9% in 1975 to 8.5% in 2013, while the 30-day prevalence of use of alcohol by 12th graders decreased from 54% in 1991 to 39.2% in 2013.

[...]

Taxation

Taxing commercial marijuana to price adolescents out of the market may also prevent many adolescents from using marijuana. Increasing the price of cigarettes through taxes can cause adolescents to stop smoking. One study of state tobacco taxes showed that every $1.00 in increased state tax could potentially result in a 5.9% decrease in past-month smoking and a 4.1% decrease in frequent smoking among US high school youth. Also, according to a meta-analysis of 112 studies on alcohol, higher taxes tend to reduce alcohol consumption among adult and teenage social drinkers as well as problem drinkers.

Time and Date Restrictions

Marijuana use, misuse, and abuse can also be addressed by instituting time and place restrictions on commercial sales and imposing liability risks on commercial marijuana retailers. For example, alcohol control measures that limit the number of days and hours that alcohol can be sold as well as restricting the location and density of alcohol outlets can help decrease alcohol consumption and consumption-related harms.

Retailer Liability

Dram shop liability laws are effective in reducing and preventing harms associated with alcohol consumption by deterring overservice of alcohol to customers. These laws allow licensed establishments such as restaurants, bars, and liquor stores that sell or serve alcohol to individuals to be held liable for any injuries or deaths that result from a customer's intoxication. Although litigation involving dram shops can be expensive and inefficient, extending dram shop liability to marijuana retailers may serve as a way to reduce marijuana use, misuse, and abuse.

Standardizing, Testing, and Monitoring Potency and Quality

Regulatory frameworks can also be developed to standardize and determine the quality of commercial marijuana to protect consumers from adulterants (e.g., pesticides, mold, mildew, toxins) and inform them of the product's potency. Similar requirements are already in place for alcohol sales. For example, federal law and agency rules require alcohol beverage labels to include the brand name, the class and type of alcohol, the alcoholic content, the name and address of the bottler or packer, the country of origin, and a disclosure of additives and sulfites. Also, the Family Smoking Prevention and Tobacco Control Act allows the US Food and Drug Administration to set standards for nicotine levels in tobacco products.

Warning Labels

Marijuana products could also be labeled to warn consumers of health risks. Tobacco products in the United States must display the surgeon general's warning about the risk of tobacco use. Labels on alcohol must also contain a specific warning about health risks. While research has shown little effect on drinking behavior from alcohol labels, tobacco labeling's impact on consumer attitudes and behaviors is more apparent.

Advertising Restrictions

Advertising restrictions can also be used to control marijuana use and protect consumers, just as they are used for alcohol and tobacco. Restricting advertisements can have profound health effects. For example, according to one study, a complete ban on alcohol advertising would result in 7,609 fewer deaths and a 16.4% drop in alcohol-related life-years lost. Current First Amendment protections for corporate speech would likely prevent advertising regulations aimed at adult consumers but would allow restrictions on advertising aimed at adolescents and children. Consideration should also be given to the impact advertising may have on communities of color and/or groups of low socioeconomic status.

Impaired Driving

Concerns about driving while impaired by marijuana can be addressed with current laws against driving under the influence or by amending those laws to include marijuana impairment. One option may be to increase "penalties for drugged driving in localities with greater accessibility to [marijuana]." Some states have adopted per se drugged driving laws, meaning that any trace of illicit drugs in a driver is considered a drugged driving violation. While such a standard may be useful when prosecuting a drugged driving case, a recent study questions the effectiveness of per se drugged driving laws in lowering traffic fatality rates. Research should be conducted on reliable and valid methods of determining marijuana impairment. Also, similar to the case with alcohol, education on marijuana use and driving should be available.

Passive Exposure

Regulatory policies should be developed to limit passive exposures to marijuana. Passive exposures can also be addressed through prohibiting use of the drug in public locations and in the presence of minor children, as well as through restricting its use in multi-unit housing to avoid smoke drifting to neighboring units. In addition, states and localities can amend existing smoke-free laws to include marijuana smoke. Also, federal and state laws regulating the use of pesticides and fertilizers and the passive exposure of workers to such chemicals and other unsafe working conditions need to be extended to individuals working for marijuana cultivators.

Monitoring and Evaluating Regulatory Schemes

Since the regulatory scheme for commercially legal marijuana is untested and involves many unknown elements, a final strategy is to monitor and evaluate the public health impact of regulations. Regulations can then be modified according to evidence regarding their effects on public health.

[...]

Action Steps

APHA believes that, in jurisdictions that legalize the commercial sale of marijuana, the preponderance of evidence supports regulating marijuana as an important public health policy.

Therefore, APHA

- Urges federal, state, and local governments to:
  - Regulate commercially legalized marijuana as a public health priority and develop, adopt, monitor, and evaluate regulatory controls for commercially legalized marijuana that reduce and prevent the drug's use, misuse, and abuse.
  - Support and fund research into the health effects of marijuana use, misuse, and abuse.
  - Coordinate their efforts to effectively regulate commercial marijuana in an effort to reduce and prevent its use, misuse, and abuse.
  - Regulate commercially legalized marijuana in partnership with state and local health departments, including the provision of resources to local and state public health agencies for the purpose of reducing and preventing marijuana's use, misuse, and abuse.
  - Tax commercial marijuana and dedicate the revenue to funding prevention, treatment, research, and regulatory frameworks to offset the costs and effects incurred

<table>
<tr><td>

FAST FACT

The Controlled Substances Act is the legal statute establishing federal drug policy in the US. It establishes the process for adding new substances to be controlled or removing controls from substances. Various parties can ask to add, delete, or change the listing of a drug or other substance.

</td></tr>
</table>

through the increased availability of marijuana and other products containing tetrahydrocannabinol (THC).

· Develop and fund standards for the quality and potency of commercial marijuana and ensure safe working conditions for those [who] cultivate marijuana.

· Exercise their authority to limit and restrict the advertising of commercial marijuana and develop required written disclosures to protect commercial marijuana consumers.

· Develop standards for determining impaired operation of motor vehicles.

· Ensure the development and availability of linguistically competent educational and informational materials for individuals with limited English proficiency.

- Calls on the federal and state governments and all federal and state agencies involved in research, policies, and programs related to marijuana to develop an evidence base regarding the public health benefits of regulating commercial marijuana.
- Calls for states that may consider legalizing commercial marijuana to refer to evidence-based regulatory controls for legalized marijuana and review and assess the regulatory frameworks of those states that have already legalized the drug.

EVALUATING THE AUTHOR'S ARGUMENTS:

This viewpoint argues that marijuana should be controlled the same way tobacco and alcohol are. Do you think those controls have been fair and effective? Would they be likely to work for marijuana? Why or why not?

Most People Think Marijuana Should Be Legalized

Pew Research Center

"Supporters of legalizing the use of marijuana are far more likely than opponents to say they have changed their mind on this issue."

The following viewpoint describes how opinions among the American public regarding legalizing marijuana have changed over time. Between 2006 and 2015—when this report was written—support for legalizing marijuana jumped dramatically. Slightly over half of those in the most recent survey favored the legal use of marijuana. The viewpoint then explores the reasons people gave for their opinion, breaking down categories based on age, race, sex, and political leaning. Since this viewpoint was published in 2015, keep in mind that attitudes about marijuana may have changed even more since then. The Pew Research Center provides information on public opinion, social issues, and demographic trends.

AS YOU READ, CONSIDER THE FOLLOWING QUESTIONS:
1. Which age groups are most and least likely to support legalizing marijuana?
2. What reasons do people give for favoring marijuana legalization?
3. What reasons do people give for wanting marijuana to remain illegal?

Public opinion about legalizing marijuana, while little changed in the past few years, has undergone a dramatic long-term shift. A new survey finds that 53% favor the legal use of marijuana, while 44% are opposed. As recently as 2006, just 32% supported marijuana legalization, while nearly twice as many (60%) were opposed.

Millennials (currently 18–34) have been in the forefront of this change: 68% favor legalizing marijuana use, by far the highest percentage of any age cohort. But across all generations—except for the Silent Generation (ages 70–87)—support for legalization has risen sharply over the past decade.

The latest national survey by the Pew Research Center, conducted March 25–29 among 1,500 adults, finds that supporters of legalizing the use of marijuana are far more likely than opponents to say they have changed their mind on this issue.

Among the public overall, 30% say they support legalizing marijuana use and have always felt that way, while 21% have changed their minds; they say there was a time when they thought it should be illegal. By contrast, 35% say they oppose legalization and have always felt that way; just 7% have changed their minds from supporting to opposing legalization.

When asked, in their own words, *why* they favor or oppose legalizing marijuana, people on opposite sides of the issue offer very different perspectives. But a common theme is the danger posed by marijuana: Supporters of legalization mention its perceived health benefits, or see it as no more dangerous than other drugs. To opponents, it is a dangerous drug, one that inflicts damage on people and society more generally.

The most frequently cited reasons for supporting the legalization of marijuana are its medicinal benefits (41%) and the belief that

Opinion on Legalizing Marijuana: 1969–2015

Do you think the use of marijuana should be made legal, or not? (%)

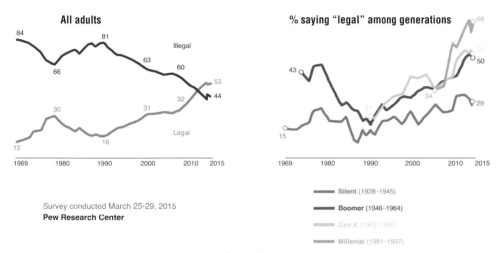

Survey conducted March 25-29, 2015
Pew Research Center

Across all generations in America, approval rates for the legalization of marijuana have increased over time.

marijuana is no worse than other drugs (36%)—with many explicitly mentioning that they think it is no more dangerous than alcohol or cigarettes.

With four states and Washington, D.C. having passed measures to permit the use of marijuana for personal use, 27% of supporters say legalization would lead to improved regulation of marijuana and increased tax revenues. About one-in-ten (12%) cite the costs and problems of enforcing marijuana laws or say simply that people should be free to use marijuana (9%).

The most frequently mentioned reason why people oppose legalization is that marijuana generally hurts society and is bad for individuals (43% say this). And while many supporters of legalization say that marijuana is less dangerous than other drugs, 30% of opponents have the opposite view: They point to the dangers of marijuana, including the possibility of abuse and addiction.

About one-in-five opponents of legalization (19%) say marijuana is illegal and needs to be policed, 11% say it is a gateway to harder drugs and 8% say it is especially harmful to young people. A small share of opponents (7%) say that while the recreational use of marijuana should be illegal, they do not object to legalizing medical marijuana.[1]

Current Opinion on Legalizing Marijuana

The pattern of opinion about legalizing marijuana has changed little in recent years. Beyond the wide generation gap in support for legalization, there continue to be demographic and partisan differences.

Majorities of blacks (58%) and whites (55%) favor legalizing marijuana, compared with just 40% of Hispanics. Men (57% favor) continue to be more likely than women (49%) to support legalization.

Nearly six-in-ten Democrats (59%) favor legalizing the use of marijuana, as do 58% of independents. That compares with just 39% of Republicans.

Both parties are ideologically divided over legalizing marijuana. Conservative Republicans oppose legalizing marijuana by roughly two-to-one (65% to 32%); moderate and liberal Republicans are divided (49% favor legalization, 50% are opposed).

Among Democrats, 75% of liberals say the use of marijuana should be legal compared with half (50%) of conservative and moderate Democrats.

Other Opinions: Federal Enforcement of Marijuana Laws

The new survey also finds that as some states have legalized marijuana—placing them at odds with the federal prohibition against marijuana—a majority of Americans (59%) say that the federal government should not enforce laws in states that allow marijuana use; 37% say that they should enforce these laws. Views on federal enforcement of marijuana laws are unchanged since the question was first asked two years ago.

In contrast to overall attitudes about the legal use of marijuana, there are only modest differences in views across partisan groups: 64% of independents, 58% of Democrats and 54% of Republicans say that the federal government should not enforce federal marijuana laws in states that allow its use.

A substantial majority of those who say marijuana should be legal (78%) do not think the federal government should enforce federal laws in states that allow its use. Among those who think marijuana should be illegal, 59% say there should be federal enforcement in states that allow marijuana use, while 38% say there should not be.

Concerns About Marijuana Use

While most Americans support legalizing marijuana, there are concerns about public use of the drug, if it were to become legal. Overall, 62% say that if marijuana were legal it would bother them if people used it in public; just 33% say this would not bother them. Like overall views of legalizing marijuana, these views have changed little in recent years.

There is less concern about the possibility of a marijuana-related business opening legally in people's own neighborhood: 57% say it would not bother them if a store or business selling marijuana opened legally in their neighborhood, while 41% say this would bother them.

And just 15% say they would be bothered if people used marijuana in their own homes; 82% say this would not bother them.

As might be expected, there are sharp differences in these concerns between people who favor and oppose legalizing marijuana. A large majority of opponents of marijuana legalization (85%) say they would be bothered by public use of the drug, if it were legal; about four-in-ten supporters (43%) also say they would be bothered by this. On the other hand, a majority of opponents of legalization (65%) say they would not be bothered if people used marijuana in their own homes; virtually all supporters of legalization (97%) would not be bothered by this.

And while 77% of those who oppose legalizing marijuana say, if it were legal, they would be bothered if a store or business selling marijuana opened in their neighborhood, just 12% of supporters of legalization say this would bother them.

About Half Say They Have Tried Marijuana

Overall, 49% say they have ever tried marijuana, while 51% say they have never done this. Self-reported experience with marijuana has shown no change over the past two years, but is higher than it was early last decade: In 2003, 38% said they had tried marijuana before, while 61% said they had not.

About a quarter of those who have tried marijuana (12% of the public overall) say they have used marijuana in the past year. Similar percentages reported using marijuana in the prior 12 months in two previous surveys, conducted in February 2014 and March 2013.

Men (56%) are 15 points more likely than women (41%) to say they have ever tried marijuana.

About half of whites (52%) and blacks (50%) say they have tried marijuana before. Among Hispanics, 36% say they have tried marijuana, while 63% say they have not.

Across generations, 59% of Baby Boomers say they've tried marijuana before; this compares with 47% of Generation Xers and 52% of Millennials. Among those in the Silent generation, only 19% say they have ever tried marijuana. Nearly a quarter of Millennials (23%) say they have used the drug in the past year, the highest share of any age cohort.

There is little difference in the shares of Democrats (48%) and Republicans (45%) who say they've tried marijuana. However, there are differences within each party by ideology. By a 61%–39% margin, most conservative Republicans say they have never tried marijuana. Among moderate and liberal Republicans, about as many say they have (52%) as have not (48%) tried marijuana before.

Among Democrats, liberals (58%) are more likely than conservatives and moderates (42%) to say they've tried marijuana.

While a majority of those who say marijuana should be legal say they've tried the drug before (65%), 34% of those who support legalization say they've never tried marijuana. Among those who say marijuana should be illegal, 29% say they have tried it before, while 71% say they have not.

Notes

1. These are volunteered responses among those who oppose legalizing marijuana. A 2013 poll found that, among the public overall, 77% said that marijuana had "legitimate medical uses."

EVALUATING THE AUTHOR'S ARGUMENTS:

This viewpoint notes that a large number of people changed their views on marijuana within a decade. What are some potential reasons for this change? Have your views changed as you have learned more about the topic? Why or why not? What might influence your views in the future?

Facts About the Legalization of Marijuana

Editor's note: These facts can be used in reports to add credibility when making important points or claims.

Talking About Marijuana

- *Cannabis:* A plant genus that has two primary species, hemp and marijuana. Both species contain CBD, but hemp has a much higher percentage of CBD and very low levels of THC compared to marijuana.
- cannabinoids: Any of a group of compounds which include the active parts of cannabis.
- CBD: Short for cannabidiol, it is one of the main components in the cannabis plant.
- hemp oil: An oil extracted from the seeds of the hemp plants. It contains no cannabinoids. Hemp oil may be used in beauty products.
- marijuana: The dried leaves, flowers, stems, and seeds from the *cannabis sativa* or *cannabis indica* plant. The plant contains the mind-altering chemical THC and other similar compounds. Marijuana can be smoked or eaten, and extracts can be made from it.
- medical marijuana: The use of marijuana with a prescription for a medical reason. Medical marijuana is not necessarily safer than marijuana acquired through other means.
- THC: Short for tetrahydrocannabinol, one of the main components in the cannabis plant. THC is responsible for most of marijuana's psychological effects. THC attaches to and activates receptors in the brain. It targets areas associated with pleasure, thinking, memory, time perception, and coordination.

Marijuana Use

Marijuana is the most commonly used illegal drug in the United States. It is used in various forms to treat medical conditions. It is also popular for recreational purposes.

The FDA approves most medications after passing a science-based evaluation. Cannabis has been approved through legislation (legal actions) rather than regulation. That means marijuana products may not have accurate labels, or any labels at all. There are no official recommendations for how much to take or when to take it. Products may not be consistent and they may have additional ingredients, which could be harmful.

Marijuana Laws

Cannabis is illegal for all uses under federal law. Federal law treats cannabis like other controlled substances, such as cocaine and heroin.

The Controlled Substances Act is the legal statute establishing federal drug policy in the United States. It sets up the process for adding new substances to be controlled, or removing controls from substances. Various parties can ask to add, delete, or change the listing of a drug or other substance. These include the Drug Enforcement Administration (DEA), the Department of Health and Human Services (HHS), the manufacturer of a drug, a medical society or association, a public interest group, and individual citizens.

The Controlled Substances Act lists marijuana as a Schedule I drug, meaning it has "no currently accepted medical use and a high potential for abuse." Other Schedule I drugs include heroin, LSD, ecstasy, meth, and peyote. The DEA does not recognize any difference between medical and recreational uses of cannabis.

While marijuana is illegal at the federal level, it is legal in some states. The first law to make cannabis legal for some uses went into effect in California in 1996. The Compassionate Use Act intended to allow marijuana use only for seriously ill patients. However, physicians could recommend marijuana under any circumstance, which led to abuse of the law. Later medical marijuana laws typically had greater controls. They narrowly defined the illnesses for which marijuana could be recommended. Some placed restrictions on growers and dispensaries.

In November 2012, citizens in Colorado and the state of Washington voted to make it legal to possess and smoke pot recreationally. Since then, additional states have made marijuana legal for medical or recreational purposes.

State marijuana laws fall into several categories. In some states, marijuana is fully legal. The minimum age for legal use is usually twenty-one. In other states marijuana is legal only for medical uses. Use may be further limited to cannabidiol (CBD), which does not typically create a high. The medical use of cannabis may be legal for children and teenagers if a licensed caregiver supervises them. Medical cannabis is legal in forty-six states.

State laws may also decriminalize marijuana. In that case, it is still illegal, but criminal penalties are lower. There may be no criminal penalties for the use and possession of modest amounts of marijuana.

In several states, marijuana is not legal under any circumstances and people may face arrest for possession, use, or sale. State laws may also control the production and sale of marijuana in various ways.

People who violate federal law by using marijuana may face serious consequences, even in states where marijuana is legal. They could be arrested and imprisoned. They may have property confiscated. Someone convicted of a felony for drug possession could be evicted from a rented home, lose his or her job, and have trouble finding future employment.

For updates on marijuana laws by state, visit Americans for Safe Access at https://www.safeaccessnow.org/state_and_federal_law.

Organizations to Contact

The editors have compiled the following list of organizations concerned with the issues debated in this book. The descriptions are derived from materials provided by the organizations. All have publications or information available for interested readers. The list was compiled on the date of publication of the present volume; the information provided here may change. Be aware that many organizations take several weeks or longer to respond to inquiries, so allow as much time as possible for the receipt of requested materials.

Center on Addiction
633 Third Ave., 19th Floor
New York, NY 10017-6706
phone: (212) 841-5200
website: www.centeronaddiction.org
The Center on Addiction is a national nonprofit that merged with the Partnership for Drug-Free Kids. The group supports families as they address substance use and addiction, from prevention to recovery. The website offers information on prevention and treatment. It provides a list of journals, books, and special reports.

DrugSense
14252 Culver Dr. #328
Irvine, CA, 92604-0326
phone: (800) 266-5759
website: www.drugsense.org/cms/
DrugSense's mission is ending drug prohibition. The website offers resources and ways to get involved. The Media Awareness Project (MAP) Drug News Archive offers a research tool to encourage unbiased media coverage.

National Institute on Drug Abuse (NIDA)
6001 Executive Blvd.
Rockville, Maryland 20852
phone: (301) 443-1124 website: www.drugabuse.gov
NIDA is part of the National Institutes of Health, which is a division of the US government. Its mission is to advance science on the causes and effects of drug use and addiction. The website has information on different drugs, prevention and treatment of abuse, current research, and news. Step-by-step guides offer information on getting treatment for a drug program.

National Organization for the Reform of Marijuana Laws (NORML)
1100 H St. NW, Suite 830
Washington, DC 20005
phone: (202) 483-5500
website: www.norml.org
email: norml@norml.org
NORML's mission is "to move public opinion sufficiently to legalize the responsible use of marijuana by adults, and to serve as an advocate for consumers to assure they have access to high quality marijuana that is safe, convenient and affordable."

Smart Approaches to Marijuana
400 N Columbus St.
Alexandria, VA, 22314
website: learnaboutsam.org/
email: info@learnaboutsam.org
This Virginia-based group is opposed to marijuana legalization. Its staff and science advisory board include experts in research, addiction, and treatment. The website provides information on marijuana and mental health, marijuana and social justice, and more. You can download a variety of fact sheets.

For Further Reading

Books

Barcott, Bruce. *Weed the People: The Future of Legal Marijuana in America*. New York, NY: Time Books, 2015. The author studies two states where marijuana is legal, Washington and Colorado. What lessons do they hold for the rest of the country?

Caulkins, Jonathan P., Beau Kilmer, and Mark A.R. Kleiman. *Marijuana Legalization: What Everyone Needs to Know*. Oxford, UK: Oxford University Press, 2016. This title discusses what is happening with marijuana policy and explores every side of the issue.

Dufton, Emily. *Grass Roots: The Rise and Fall and Rise of Marijuana in America*. New York, NY: Basic Books, 2017. This book tells the story of marijuana in America, from acceptance to demonization to growing acceptance again.

Goldstein, Margaret J. *Legalizing Marijuana: Promises and Pitfalls*. Minneapolis, MN: Twenty-First Century Books, 2016. Learn about the movement to legalize marijuana and the arguments on each side.

Hudak, John. *Marijuana: A Short History (The Short Histories)*. Washington, DC: Brookings Institution Press, 2016. The author explores the politics and policies surrounding marijuana in the US and around the world.

Lee, Martin A. *Smoke Signals: A Social History of Marijuana—Medical, Recreational and Scientific*. New York, NY: Scribner, 2013. This title explores the role cannabis has played in American history. The author is in favor of legalization.

Nelson, Julie. *Marijuana's Harmful Effects on Youth (Marijuana Today)*. Broomall, PA: Mason Crest Publishers, 2018. Learn how marijuana affects the human body and brain, including benefits and harmful effects.

Ventura, Marne. *The Debate About Legalizing Marijuana (Focus Readers: Pros and Cons: Voyager Level)*. Mendota Heights, MN: Focus Readers, 2018. Get an overview of the notable pros and cons of legalizing marijuana.

Ventura, Marne. *Legalizing Marijuana (Debating the Issues)*. New York, NY: Weigl Publishers, 2019. Explore the issues surrounding the legalization of marijuana. The book includes multimedia content and an educational activity.

Periodicals and Internet Sources

"Against Drug Prohibition," ACLU. https://www.aclu.org/other /against-drug-prohibition.

Bendici, Ray, "Campuses Cope with Increased Marijuana Legalization," *University Business*, Vol. 21, No. 8, August 2018. https://university business.com/college-campuses-cope-with-increased-marijuana -legalization/.

Benyamin, Chaya, "Should We Legalize Marijuana?" *Perspective*, 2018. https://www.theperspective.com/debates/living/should-we -legalize-marijuana/.

Blake, Brian, "State-Level Marijuana Legalization: Myths and Facts," Hudson Institute, Inc., November 13, 2015. https:// www.hudson.org/research/11904-state-level-marijuana -legalization-myths-and-facts.

Blankstein, Andrew, "Foreign Cartels Embrace Home-Grown Marijuana in Pot-Legal States," *NBC News*, May 29, 2018. https:// www.nbcnews.com/news/us-news/foreign-cartels-embrace -home-grown-marijuana-pot-legal-states-n875666.

Caulkins, Jon, "Nip It in the Bud: Could Donald Trump Be Our Best Hope for Sensible Marijuana Legalization?" *Washington Monthly*, Vol. 49, No. 1–2, January–February 2017. https:// washingtonmonthly.com/magazine/januaryfebruary -2017/nip-it-in-the-bud/.

Gavura, Scott, "Medical Marijuana: Where Is the Evidence?" *Science Based Medicine*, January 11, 2011. https://sciencebasedmedicine .org/medical-marijuana-where-is-the-evidence/.

Grinspoon, Peter, "Medical Marijuana," *Harvard Health Blog*, January 15, 2018. https://www.health.harvard.edu/blog/medical -marijuana-2018011513085.

Kabir, Sumaiya, "20 Medical Benefits of Marijuana You Probably Never Knew," *Lifehack*, August 22, 2018. https://www.lifehack.org/articles /lifestyle/20-medical-benefits-marijuana-you-probably-never-knew .html.

Khazan, Olga, "The Surprising Effect of Marijuana Legalization on College Students," *Atlantic*, June 16, 2017. https://www.theatlantic .com/health/archive/2017/06/marijuana-legalization-college -students/530607/.

"Medical Marijuana," Parkinson Foundation. https://parkinson.org /Understanding-Parkinsons/Treatment/Medical-Marijuana.

Newman, Katclyn, "Study: Marijuana Policies Not Increasing Teen Use," *US News*, February 15, 2019. https://www.usnews.com/news /best-states/articles/2019-02-15/marijuana-policies-not -associated-with-increased-teen-use-study-says.

Peoples Stokes, Crystal, "People of Color Were Targeted by the War on Drugs. They Must Benefit from Marijuana Legalization," *Newsweek*, May 3, 2019. https://www.newsweek.com/people -color-marijuana-legalization-opinion-1381990.

Rauch, Jonathan, "It's All in the Implementation: Why Cannabis Legalization Is Less Like Marriage Equality and More Like Health Care Reform," *Washington Monthly*, March–May 2014. https:// washingtonmonthly.com/magazine/marchaprilmay-2014 /its-all-in-the-implementation/.

Sullum, Jacob, "Does Legalization Boost Teen Marijuana Use?" *Reason*, May 2017. https://reason.com/2017/04/20/does -legalization-boost-teen-m/.

Terrell, Jessica, "Marijuana Legalization and Its Impact on Schools," *District Administration,* January 2017. https://districtadministra- tion.com/marijuana-legalization-and-its-impact-on-schools/.

Trilling, David, "Marijuana Legalization: Tax Revenue and Changing Consumption," *Journalist's Resource*, August 8, 2016. https:// journalistsresource.org/studies/economics/taxes/marijuana -legalization-tax-revenue-changing-consumption/.

"What Is Marijuana?" National Institute on Drug Abuse, June 2018. https://www.drugabuse.gov/publications/drugfacts/marijuana.

Websites

Citizens Against Legalizing Marijuana (CALM)

(https://calmca.org)

Citizens Against Legalizing Marijuana hopes to stop the spread of marijuana distribution and use. It asks state, county, and local governments to work within current federal law.

Marijuana Policy Project (MPP)

(www.mpp.org)

The MPP believes that the greatest harm associated with marijuana is imprisonment. The group focuses on removing criminal penalties for marijuana use, and on making marijuana medically available to people who have the approval of their doctors.

Students for Sensible Drug Policy (SSDP)

(www.ssdp.org)

The SSDP is an international network of students concerned about the consequences of the war on drugs on society. SSDP tries to bring young people together for honest conversations about drugs and drug policy.

Index

dispensaries, 17, 18, 45, 67, 68, 69, 71, 84, 109

dopamine, 59, 62

driving under the influence of alcohol, 9, 11, 14, 98

driving under the influence of marijuana, 11, 14, 70, 93, 98

Drug Enforcement Administration (DEA), 7, 14, 76, 87, 88, 89, 90, 109

E

ecstasy (methylenedioxy-methamphetamine), 14, 60, 88, 109

edibles, 8, 41, 44, 48, 53, 55, 56

Ekins, Gavin, 26

extracts, 7, 41–42, 44, 53, 55, 56, 57, 108

F

felony drug offenses and convictions, 8, 78, 80, 110

Fergusson, David, 36–37

Food and Drug Administration (FDA), 19, 54, 83, 84, 85, 89, 97, 109

Foster, William H., 82

Frey, Chris, 66

G

gateway drugs, 19, 31, 32–37, 38, 47, 103

guns and firearms, 52, 70, 79–80

H

hallucinations, 9, 43, 46, 48, 52

Harris, Richard, 16

hash oil, 41, 53, 55, 56–57

hemp, 7, 108

heroin, 7, 14, 17, 24, 34, 37, 60, 62, 70, 88, 109

Hockenberry, Jason, 18

I

incarceration, 8, 22, 29, 76, 78, 79, 110

Institute of Medicine, 32, 38

L

learning, 9, 14–15, 40, 43

Levitan, Dave, 31

LSD (lysergic acid diethylamide), 7, 14, 88, 109

M

marijuana, cost of, 66, 69, 99–100, 103

marijuana use, 7, 8, 9, 12, 14, 15, 18, 19, 21, 22, 23, 24, 31, 32, 35, 36, 37, 38, 40, 41, 43, 44, 45, 46, 47, 48, 49, 50, 54, 55, 57, 67, 94, 96–97, 98, 99, 102, 104, 105, 109

Medicaid, 18, 19

medical marijuana, 8, 9, 16, 17, 18, 19, 20, 24, 27, 52, 74, 75–77, 78, 79–82, 83, 84–86, 88, 94, 104, 108, 109, 110

Medicare, 17, 18

memory, 9, 11, 14–15, 40, 43, 45, 95, 108

Méndez, Sam, 87

meth (methamphetamine), 7, 14, 60, 109

Picture Credits